'Community at Heart'

'Who Will Bury our Dead?'

by

Marie O'Connell

Best wishes
I hope you enjoy my
Book ☺

Marie OConnell

♡

In Dedication

This book is dedicated to the most important people in my life. To my mum and dad Brid and Patrick O'Connell my greatest influences. My children Tara, Niall and Niamh, my greatest love. My brother Pat my greatest ally. My sisters Claire and Clodagh my greatest delight. My partner Kerry my greatest joy.

In Memory

It is written in loving memory of my gorgeous mother Brid who I loved with all my heart. She loved her community and contributed all her life especially to her beloved choir.

In Thanks

Writing a book is something I always wanted to do. It is harder than I thought but more rewarding than I could ever have imagined. None of this would have been possible without my work in the Diocese of Killaloe. Thank you to all the communities I came in contact with and to the colleagues I worked with.

I am eternally grateful to all my Pierce uncle's Mike, Pat, Tom, James, John and remembering Simon who I never met and my O'Connell uncle's Michael, Lawrence and Thomas you were all gentlemen. To my Pierce Aunts, Mamie, Kathleen, Ellen, Pauline and to Mags my inspiration. To my O'Connell aunt's Margaret, Kitty and Anna, your beauty and grace astounds me to this day. To the Pierce and O'Connell cousins, you are a great bunch and I love you all. To my lovely nieces and nephews Laura, Rachel, Ciara, Cathal, Eoin, Anna and Bobby you are our future.

A very special thanks to my friends who have held me together over the years. To my long-time friends Ena, Grainne, Geraldine, Maura, Therese, Shirley, and Jane, you sustained me in ways I never knew I needed and my newer friends Liz, Roisin, Carmel, Carol, Sandra, and Theresa, thank you for the never-ending wine and whine. To my work colleagues in University of Limerick especially Dee, Mamie, Eimear, Emily and Carmel, the next book is about you.

To my writers group the Killaloe Hedge School especially to David and Kathleen. Your encouragement, support and vision helped me bring my book to being.

Writing this book about the story of community is a dream come true for me. I am forever indebted to Dr Conor Reidy, Silver View Editing for his editorial help, keen insight, and encouragement. It is because of your efforts and encouragement that I have a legacy to pass on to my family.

Thank you to the men in my life, I am blessed with the best father in the world, the best partner in the world, the best brother in the world and the best son in the world. To the ladies in my life, my sisters, the best a girl could ask for and my daughters who never caused me any trouble. I will never know how you survived me as your mother.

To all the Pointe Vecchio crew -you -nourish my soul.

Pointe Vecchio Kilaloe – my sustanince

8

Table of Contents

Foreword

I can never forget a certain parish of which I once was a member. Community? Forget it. People came trotting in to 'get' Mass, and then hurried off with hardly a nod to anyone. The priest mumbled and muttered his way through the Mass, and then disappeared through a door behind the altar. No way did he ever come out to the front door to greet anyone. That was our 'church'.

That was then. This is now. And Marie O'Connell tells us about another kind of church.

Church is community, she insists. Her wonderful book begins by describing the community in Broadford where she grew up. It was truly a community, where people cared for one another, through relationships, sport, bereavement, child care, schooling, motherhood and fatherhood, everything.

Now Marie wants something like that to happen again. But not a nostalgic return to the past, which anyhow is gone forever. For the church, as we know it, is in deepest trouble. Priests are few, and aging— mostly over 70. Soon there will be none in many places. And many of the pews in our churches are empty.

So what do we do? Some say the church is dead or dying. But we ourselves are the church, and we are certainly not dead. We simply have to change our notion of church, and realise that it is community. So we create community. It does not have to be in a gothic building with pointed arches, which probably will be impossible to heat, anyhow. Much of the new kind of community will be in homes, around tables, which Marie calls 'tabling'.

This marvellous book tells us how to create such a community, and the key, Marie says, is caring for one another. Layfolk doing the caring, not the priest (who most likely will no longer be here). So layfolk have to begin to reach out, as never before, to the lonely, the bereaved, the sick, the vulnerable, the young. Maintenance must give way to mission and thus to ministry. We layfolk must realise that we have a vocation, just as much as any priest, and that vocation is to love. No more; no less. The Priesthood of the Laity.

The change for all this to happen will be drastic, but necessary. It will mean layfolk—both women and men— ministering to the sick, conducting funerals and church services, reaching out to the youth, creating a welcoming community, developing social life, volunteering one's talents, working through pastoral councils—the book contains a list of functions and it is a long list indeed.

But the key to it all is the development of spirituality in all of us, without which everything is meaningless.

So who is this Marie O'Connell, who tells us all this? She is a person of considerable experience, indeed of authority, with a degree in Theology and a post grad in community education, who has spent five long years as Pastoral Visitor to the parishes of the Diocese of Killaloe—one of the largest dioceses in Ireland.

It involved meeting with pastoral councils all over the diocese, speaking at Mass in churches everywhere—a woman speaking in church!—but above all, in learning from both layfolk and clergy where lie the problems and their solutions.

There are some quite wonderful ideas in this book, about women deacons, bringing the denominations together (why not?), how families and roles are changing, how to face the decline in togetherness and what to do about it, introducing Celtic spirituality, how to create effective pastoral councils.

But above all, this book is about building community, the key to which is caring for one another. The guidance and advice here is practical and full of hope. And it will be all up to the laity, for there won't be any priests, or very few anyhow.

Marie has the backing of Pope Benedict, in all of what she says. She quotes him as saying that the Church 'needs a mature and committed laity, able to make its specific contribution to the mission of the Church.'

This is a book about just that, one which could change parishes and dioceses around Ireland, and might well be the saving.

David Rice · March 2022

David Rice is a member of of The National Union of Journalists and author: Shattered Vows (London: Michael Joseph/ Penguin; New York: William Morrow Inc; Triumph Books; St Louis: Ligouri Press; Belfast: Blackstaff Press); The Dragon's Brood - Conversations with Young Chinese (London: HarperCollins); Blood Guilt (Belfast: Blackstaff Press); The Rathmines Stylebook (Dublin: Folens); Song of Tiananmen Square (Brandon/Mt Eagle); Kirche ohne Priester (Munich: Bertelsmann; Goldmann Verlag); The Pompeii Syndrome (Cork: Mercier Press); La Sindrome di Pompei (Rome: Newton Compton); The Joy of Looking (Keeper Books); Look & Grow Mindful (Keeper Books); I Will Not Serve (Dublin: Red Stag); Corduroy Boy (Dublin: Red Stag); Yes, You Can Write (Dublin: Red Stag); The Little Roads of Ireland (Dublin: Red Stag)

Introduction

'I bring you with reverent hands The books of my numberless dreams.'
W.B.Yeats

Introduction

The idea for this book came about after visiting parishes across the Diocese of Killaloe, which comprises of counties Clare, North Tipperary parts of Limerick and Offaly. Dramatic changes taking place in our communities and family frameworks were very noticeable. The book will examine changes that took place over the past one hundred years since Ireland achieved independence (1921-2021).

Our change was radical. Most notably, there was a change in economic and social situations. In each chapter, the reader is introduced to a wealth of new and old information as well as insight into our communities. The intention is to address the possible gaps in the community of contemporary Ireland by focusing on the challenges facing our rural communities and those who live there. The book concentrates on the experience and understanding of research as well as gatherings across these communities. It brings together stories and experiences interwoven with research. While the themes selected are wide-ranging, together they explore what it is to be 'the heart of the community'. This work is intended to throw light on key aspects of community living.

It has been a pleasure to work with Parish Pastoral Councils, community groups and individuals who strongly and passionately believe in their community. Their shared outlook and vision is one of respect for each other at a time when many in the community have become disillusioned and filled with doubt. This book reviews some of the forces that shaped our communities.

It pulls together concerns that indicate where we are and where we hope to go.
It is a summing up of the current challenges and responses, the questions asked and the search for answers.

The ideas I present address a variety of issues encountered while working with pastoral councils over the years. I am not setting myself up as an expert, but I am hoping my experiences will succeed in generating discussion and debate. I believe in people. I believe in their ability to recognise their reality. This book will document major challenges confronting community in Ireland. I have been most fortunate to work with people who believe they are ordinary but they are extraordinary, nonetheless, their voices are not heard. These people are creative thinkers who continue to overcome adversity. It would be fantastic if these thinkers were allowed to unleash their creativity. I am an advocate of hope and believe in taking a positive view of the future. Perhaps it would be a good idea to begin at the very beginning, as Julie Andrews says, in the sound of music, it is a very good place to start.

Begin with men, women, voluntary groups, community groups. As a society, we have been through a tough time. At the risk of over-simplification, maybe we just need to begin with ourselves, with our purpose. Can we rediscover our meaning? May we look once more to our traditions, our roots, our spirituality, our community, and our family? Shall we explore a new vision for the future? I love meeting people and I welcome every opportunity to engage and connect with them. Life always brought challenges, but today's world is particularly challenging. For me, life is about helping others, making a positive difference.

Family and life in Ireland always centred around community and being there for one another. Reaching out without expecting anything in return, 'we don't need to do great things we just need to do small things with great love'. I worked with the Diocese of Killaloe, I loved it. I used my voice to the best of my ability. I held meetings all over the diocese where large numbers were in attendance. People shared their innovative ideas but when it came to action it was difficult to get support. Like many other women who have active roles in the Church community, I found it difficult to find my niche. Having the title of Pastoral Worker did have its credence and entitled me to sit within the higher echelons, but it did not help when it came to decision making. I felt listened to, but I did not feel heard.

I come from a small community called Broadford in East Clare, not unlike similar communities dotted around Ireland. For me, Broadford was a place of belonging, a place where I developed my identity. It was a place I felt heard. I was a child who was loved, listened to and I knew I belonged. In my family, I felt protected and safe. Through our rituals and traditions, we were always a living community. We had a sense of belonging.

I left Broadford and travelled extensively but every time I return, I know I am home. My mother was always one for the sayings and she always said 'home is where the heart is', and my heart is in Broadford with its traditions, its rituals and its lovely people. As a child, I used to write little stories and hand them out to friends and family. I have now written this book and dedicate it to my family, friends, and community but most of all to the memory of my mother. When I embarked on this writing journey my mother was alive. Now as I write it, she keeps popping into my head.

She was a huge influence on my life. This was something I recognised and admitted to while she was alive, but now that she is gone, I hear and feel her in all aspects of my life. I attempted several times to pen this book but procrastinated.

After the shock passing of my mum, I wanted some way of honouring her memory. Finally, I decided to pursue my lifelong dream of writing a book and remember my mother's love of her Church and her community. What better place to start, therefore, than my community. In the past, I wrote newspaper articles and short stories for my writing group. A book would be a whole new undertaking.Taking into consideration my experiences as a Pastoral Worker and the knowledge gained from my involvement in communities, I hope you enjoy this book. I have been blessed with the experience I gained. I enjoy sharing that experience.

Communities have changed throughout my lifetime, yet so many things stay the same. I look at the changing face of communities over the decades. I am fully aware that many will disagree with my considerations, but this is what makes it all worthwhile. In many ways, opening a discussion is what is important. This book is not about changing your core beliefs, it is about beginning a conversation. Try to avoid the tendency to be defensive and keep away from statements like 'that would never work for us.' To unearth the community we want, we will need to push ourselves out of our comfort zones. By changing, we are not dishonouring our past we are merely changing how we do things into the future. We need to know where we came from to know where we are going. People are becoming disconnected from the communities that shaped them. Maybe it is time to face our fears and move from talking to doing.

Say farewell to the status quo and begin somewhere to create the community we want. This book looks at how we can make a difference. It explores obstacles to effective leadership and attempts to offer guidelines in overcoming them. I ask you while reading it, to be open to change. Be open to your memories of the past and be open to an imaginative way forward.

Chapter one

Story: Tradition and Spirit

*"The only good thing to do with good advice is to
pass it on; it is never of any use to oneself."*
Oscar Wilde

Our story as community

In the words of William Butler Yeats', 'all is changed, changed utterly'. If our grandparents were around today, they would think that all had changed utterly. It is hoped we will learn from the mistakes of our past and with any hope a terrible beauty may be born. With the fast pace of life, we are beginning to replace participation in the community with a service delivery approach. Are we tearing the heart out of the community and voluntary sector? Most ordinary Irish people are focusing on surviving the day-to-day effects of austerity. They are not aware that valuable structures within the community are disintegrating. Community means many things to many people at different times in their life.

I have spent most of my life reading about and working in the community. We have a variety of communities in our lives, such as our family, our locality, our spiritual community. We have our individual experiences. It is about a sense of belonging coming from our roots, from where we are comfortable. It is about welcome, connectedness, support, and respect. We all need support at some point in our lives. Having grown up in a small rural community, it was difficult when I left there to embrace another community. That was until I made my home in Ballina/Killaloe, a place that has brought me great joy and peace.

Even though I left Broadford at the age of nineteen to go to work in Dublin, I remained connected to my community of origin.
Thirty years on I still feel connected to Broadford even though I have my own family with our connections in our new community. I have friends and family still living in Broadford and every time I

return there, I feel enveloped by the sense of belonging and connectedness.

My family has been rooted in County Clare for at least two centuries. Most of us here in Ireland know where we are rooted, and we feel that sense of belonging.

Recently I attended a funeral of a very well-known local man. I did not know him, but I knew two of his sons. This funeral was a real celebration of the man's life. Sitting in the church during this celebration I could feel the love and appreciation of his influence. It was obvious the celebrant knew him and his family very well. Every reading, prayer, hymn, song, music, and speech was chosen with him in mind. This man lived ninety-seven years of what seemed a very fulfilled life. He was born in a small townland in the parish of Feakle in County Clare. While sitting in the church absorbing everything going on, I got a sense of real community. A sense of where we come from and what we are about. A sense of how we appreciate our neighbours and their journey in life. I was struck by the stories and memories of the man and his long life.

Although he never left the tiny area where he was born other than to perform his business as a cattle dealer, he seemed to have a global view of life. His story was a great example of who we are as a people. I sat there mostly paying attention, but my mind wandered to how life must have changed for him over his ninety-seven years. I thought about how we could all learn from him. The memory that struck me most was one of joy, respect, fulfilment, and most of all love. A deep, surviving love. We heard about how Johnny (not his real name) went to Limerick to sell a cow. With the money he received, he bought a watch for his wife, the great Molly (not her real name).

Molly wore that watch until the day she died at which point Johnny wore the watch until the day he died.

This is love as it should be, not the romantic love of candlelight and creating a big gesture but the undying respect of one person for another. The memories shared at this funeral were of a couple who enjoyed a relationship we all long for and to which we aspire. They were of a man who lived to the full even though he did not have the great holidays, the big house, the big car, he had something much, much more. He enjoyed life, experienced great love, was blessed with a large loving family and judging by the number of people attending his funeral he was adored by great neighbours.

The simplicity of this funeral together with the memories imparted demonstrated how we as Irish people have a great story. This was a story Johnny lived and demonstrated to the full. Born in the early-1900s, he saw Ireland change almost beyond recognition from his young days, yet he had an excellent handle on life. Listening to his narrative it struck me that Johnny knew all about mindfulness before it ever became a thing. He lived until he died. He was lucky to have a large family who went on to live their lives all the while remembering where they came from and the solid foundation they had from Johnny and the great Molly.

We are a fantastic country when it comes to death, and we rally around the bereaved, doing everything in our power to comfort and support them. We know of tragedies that occur in our communities and how we come together to support those affected.

Regardless of the changes our society is going through we are amazing when our neighbours need us, and they are amazing when we need them.
I can attest to this as recently, when my mother passed way too soon, our neighbours were phenomenal.

St Mary's Church Feakle, Co. Clare
(Photo Marie O'Connell)

St Peters Church Broadford. My Church.
(Photo Marie O'Connell)

Our story of Broadford

Broadford, my community, my heart my soul. There is something special about every community, the fields, the woodlands, the mountains, the hills. Maybe it is a river, a lake, a get-it-done attitude, or an everyone-is-welcome ethos. Whether these are places, traditions, or mindsets, the community characteristics are what matter to people. They bring the community together and help them care about where they live. Encouraging people to engage helps connect individuals with what they love most about their community. It transforms personal and emotional connections into a plan that serves as the basis for future community decisions. Encouraging people in the community to participate in local decision-making empowers them to shape the future of where they live.

I believe Broadford has a unique character which I love. Like most villages in Ireland and especially Clare, Broadford has its features, attributes, and qualities. Broadford – or Áth Leathan in Irish – is a small village in East Clare. Áth Leathan means a wide ford in the river. It is tucked into the Glenomra Valley on the slopes of the Slieve Bearnagh Mountains near Doon Lough. The parish is in the Diocese of Killaloe. It originated in the medieval parishes of Kilseily and Killokennedy. Part of Killokennedy was amalgamated with Kilseily to form what is now the parish of Broadford. The parish today has three church buildings, in Broadford, Kilbane and Kilmore.

I no longer live in Broadford, but I am there very often. My family still live there and have done for centuries. It is where my roots are.

I feel Broadford always gives me back my spirit, my sense of belonging even when times are tough.
Like most Irish communities, it is full of local pride especially when it comes to supporting our local and county sports teams. I will never forget the celebrations after Clare won the All-Ireland hurling final for the first time in eighty years. The celebrations lasted for months.

I love Broadford because the people you meet there become your family. It is a great place to have children and raise a family. I loved growing up there with the various community groups providing us with places to go and talents to nourish.
My mother and father were involved in community building. Mum was involved in the formation of the ICA (Irish Countrywomen's Association) over fifty years ago and even in these modern times it still exists.

My Dad was involved in the community hall where he organised live music dances every weekend. It was a buzzing community. When I was in my teens, I helped with the formation of a new youth club. We had great leaders from the community and were seen as a shining example to other youth clubs around the county. If you enjoy people, as my parents did, being involved in the community was an amazing opportunity to spend time with people.

When you are out and about in the community you will hear incredible stories if you are willing to listen. Of course, you need to take some stories with a pinch of salt as many tales released into the community grow legs. A friend once told me how she particularly disliked being involved in groups, but she loved grabbing a cuppa with people, hearing their stories, and knowing what was going on in the community.

I loved being involved. I love people and I love trying to figure out ways to support those that need it, by connecting them to other people. When you get involved in building the community, you have the chance to provide something to society that is fundamental to human happiness. It helps provide a place of trust, connectedness and belonging. Being surrounded by trusted human beings in our communities is a deep, profound need.

Small village communities are great places of care. That is not to say they are perfect. Indeed, in Broadford, there was often tension over divisive decisions made in certain groups. It is not always possible to make everyone happy and small communities are very often like families, when you are so close there is sometimes division.

Communities have changed over the years with many young people leaving to pursue their dreams. Broadford lost so many young people to unemployment in the 1980s but in recent years they began to move back, while the younger cohort is beginning to move away again. This is a pull of our roots and grounding.

In today's progressively disconnected and divided world, it is easier than ever to feel lonely and alone as well as to doubt people's intentions around us, but small supportive communities can nourish the soul. It is wonderful to get together to provide people with a place of belonging, space and time to feel connected and less lonely. A space to feel valued. By getting involved in our community we have the possibility of changing people's lives. Although no longer living in Broadford I feel those of us that lived there in our teens helped in building a vibrant community. I know I made lifelong friendships in Broadford. Friends I have to this day, friends I have laughed and cried with.

I remember it as being a vibrant happy place. We were very focused on our traditions and valued the spirit of our ancestors. Unfortunately, like most of our rural communities, Broadford has been a victim of the fall in populations and a shortage of priests, something that is not about religion but about what it represents. Throughout the country, the prospect of church closures is being raised.

With an approximate population of 800, in pre-Famine days Broadford is reported to have had 8,000 inhabitants. This is very difficult to believe. The twenty-first century is a different age with different needs; however, we continue to need connectedness, a feeling of belonging, a feeling of place, somewhere we can lay our hat.

The wonders of the wider world are totally within our grasp in today's modern world in terms of communication and travel. It would be a shame, however, to lose the wonders that surround us in our local communities. It is a joy to discover the history of our locality and the story of who went before us.

The story of Ireland, County Clare and Broadford is rich and varied. Each generation naturally feels their time is the most important and most unique but many went before us. Looking to our surroundings and our history is essential to understanding all who went before. This includes those who passed on their traditions, customs, and spirit. Although a traditional Catholic parish, Broadford was always highly valued by those living there whether practising, non-practising, believer, or non-believer. The parochial church, school and community hall remain at the heart of community life even if the notion of community undergoes great transformation. Broadford is a relatively new parish in historical terms.

One of the earliest references to a parish chapel at Broadford comes from a report in 1812 when Fr Matthew Corbett, the then parish priest was attacked inside the thatched building by invaders during an agrarian flare-up. The next we hear about this building is when in 1836 the parish priest Fr Peter Curtain replaced the thatched building with the present St. Peter's Church. It is thought that the site may be different.

It is a cruciform building that usually depicts a church built with a layout developed in Gothic architecture, in a cruciform or cross shape. This is a design feature developed for the Killaloe Diocese. One of my abiding memories is the carving of St Peter on the wall at the entrance to the church. We told him all our secrets. It is thought that this eighteenth-century carving comes from earlier times.Over the years, St Peter's was renovated several times.

One of my favourite churches in the Diocese of Killaloe is the church in Kilmore. St Joseph's was built circa 1822 and is believed to have cost £150. This building is reputed to be the smallest in the Diocese. It seems it was originally thatched and used as a schoolhouse. It was slated in 1850 with the most recent renovations carried out in 1994. This church has a congregation that wants to maintain its traditions, but this is becoming increasingly less likely as the number of priests is declining. I do not doubt that this community, although small, will rise to the challenge and help their church survive in some manner.

It is reported that a thatched church was also built in Kilbane in 1739, however, it is uncertain where. Another church was built in 1815. This in turn was replaced by St Mary's in the late 1830s.

It is a large cruciform church built in a similar form to that of St Peter's church in Broadford. Fr John Bourke a parish priest in Kilbane in 1859 organised a lottery, an idea well ahead of time, and this was used to refurbish the church. The community in Kilbane is very proud of their church and I have no doubt they will take care of it well into the future. Both Kilbane and Kilmore have now been closed by the diocese but I am confident they will survive into the future.

In the parish of Broadford, there are some notable historical events connected to the lovely churches. The parish priest in Broadford in 1796 was Fr Terence O'Shaughnessy; he was in Paris during the French revolution. In 1828, Tom Steele visited to warn against the forming of secret societies.

This warning came in the wake of Daniel O'Connell's great victory in the County Clare election. Broadford in the 1850s was one of the key parishes in East Clare involved in the tenant-right agitation. Daniel Vaughan, a significant human rights agitator, was from Kilbane. He was appointed Bishop of Killaloe in 1851 and served for eight years.

Daniel's nephew, also Daniel Vaughan was famous in America as a scientist, mathematician, physiologist, and astronomer. Born in Kilbane circa 1818, Daniel received his early education at the local hedge school and later attended the Killaloe classical school. He emigrated to the United States around 1840 and became a member of the American Association for the Advancement of Science and was in great demand on the lecture circuit.

Another historical feature is a holy well near the old church at Kilokennedy whose waters are reputed to give strength to babies.

In Clare, we were brought up with the spirit of the people that went before us. Their ideas, their customs, their beliefs, form who we are. These cultural traditions are in the stories our ancestors told.

Tradition is part of our DNA and nowhere is tradition more alive, more colourful, and more vibrant than in County Clare. I often return to Broadford to take time to feel the energy of our bygone culture and fuel my heart and soul. I agree with RS Thomas, a poet and priest noted for his spirituality when he said 'we only know who we are by knowing where we are.

A particular place creates around us a unique culture, that gives us not only our identity but also our vision and values'. According to him our sense of heritage is fundamentally linked to our sense of identity. This is what Broadford means for me, as the saying goes 'you can take the girl out of Broadford, but you cannot take Broadford out of the girl'.

Broadford surrounded us with so much history, heritage, and nature. The river flowing through the village was a great favourite but one of our preferred hang-out places was Doon Lake about a mile outside the village. That was a time when we could meet up as young teenagers and wander the roads and byways without fear or anxiety.

It was a lovely time to grow up. We explored daily, checking out the ruins of Doon House, associated with JP Holland who was the man renowned for inventing the submarine. Wherever you live you will have similar landscapes and traditions that helped form you. We explored the site of the church of Ireland built in 1811 but demolished in the 1950s.

We walked all the roads finding all sorts of treasures, quarry's, mediaeval sites, graveyards, and holy wells.

It is reported that there is a deserted miner's village beside the quarry in Kilseily but we never managed to locate it. As young teenagers, Hurdlestown House was a favourite with myself and my friends. The waterfall in the river was stunning and the overgrown gardens were so much fun to explore and stimulate our imaginations. It was a compact stone-built shooting lodge, with gables and a steeply pitched roof that was designed for Colonel White in 1871.

In my late teens, this house was renovated, and I was lucky enough to see it. It is so beautiful and has had different owners over the years. The old RIC Barracks still stands and is inhabited. I can remember the old courthouse, but it has now gone, as is the Black Horse Inn, a pub where many a story was told and retold.

The old school was located on what was known as the former Fair Green. As young people, the old school operated as a place where we could hire bikes for 10p an hour what fun we had on these machines.

The primary school is now to the south of the village. It was recently renovated and looks resplendent, beside the river. Next to the school is the community hall. Built during the 1940s, the roof and floor were taken from the Doon House ballroom. There was so much nourishment for the heart and soul in that hall over the years.

We were surrounded by woods, with Ballymaloney woods three miles east of the village reputed to be over a thousand years old. We even had an enchanted lake.

We had the house of O'Donovan, the first survey historian and archaeologist in Ireland. One thing I didn't know we had, was the house of the 'Broadford Soviet'. This I stumbled on when I was reading for this book. I never heard of the 'Broadford Soviet' and I can understand why as it appears to have split the community, pitting neighbour against neighbour.

The 'Broadford Soviet' is said to have begun in February 1922 and only lasted a few months. It consisted of the take-over of a landlord's estate in Broadford by a group of labourers and tenants. Those involved wanted change and they wanted it immediately.

Republicans did not want to accept the Anglo-Irish Treaty because they felt it betrayed the Republic. Free Staters felt it gave the nation time to achieve freedom and the socialist minority felt it killed the prospect of establishing the Workers' Republic. Broadford was not isolated in its Bolshevism as the 'Castleconnell Soviet' was made up of Irish Transport Union workers. Ballyneety had its 'Land soviet' and Mungret demanded that a large estate was divided among the parishioners.

So, it was not too unusual when on the night of 22 February 1922, Jack Kennedy, son of Martin Kennedy the balladeer, was accompanied by a group of men who broke down the door of a tenant farmers' meeting and announced that they were taking over the 'Going' estate in Broadford. I am amazed by this as I knew Jack very well in his old age and he was such a quiet man.

The 'Going' estate comprised of over 300 acres and had twenty-six tenant farmers. The rental books for 1922 showed that tenants were seriously in arrears with their payments.

For Violet Hill estate, alone, the nine tenants had paid only £71 out of a total rental of £350.

It is reported that a land agent lost his motor car and then his motorbike while trying to collect rents. Whatever hope he had of collecting rents from the tenants before the estate was apprehended by Jack and his new group, he now had little or no hope of collecting it.

The group put forward demands for a reduction in rents and the distribution of lands to the small tenants. I learned they later proposed to let lands for tillage to landless men in Broadford and to place one of their members in possession of the Lodge at Violet Hill House. During the late spring and summer, the committee made its presence felt.

It was a time of unease as neighbour was pitted against neighbour. In the end, it was the transfer of animals from one place to another that led to the premature breaking up of the Soviet.

It is reported that a local man named Paddy Donnellan burst into a meeting. He told them 'there was no way that he was going to allow any member of the Committee to lay a hand on a friend and neighbour of his'. The committee had turned cattle belonging to his neighbour John Lacy out on the road. He told the committee that he went to 'gaol before over land and he would do the gallows for them'.

It sounds to me like Broadford was an interesting place back then. Eventually, civic guards took up residence in the RIC Barracks and a modicum of peace returned to the area.

The true spirit of Bolshevism inspired the men of Broadford and was significant enough to earn them a place in the history of the Irish soviet movement of that period.

Growing up in a community with such history and spirit can only be inspirational and motivating. We are very lucky in Ireland to have such heritage. I speak about Broadford as it is where my spirit was formed. I mention Jack Kennedy because I remember him well. I remember him in his older life as he was a great friend of my grandfathers and he had card games at his house where storytelling was paramount.

Looking back now I am so glad I knew Jack and my grandfather – they were the spirit of Broadford. I am sure you can look to your area and discover your heart and soul.

Jack Kennedy son of Martin Kennedy bard of Violet Hill and treasurer of 'The Broadford Soviet' (Family photo)

Our story of Spirit – Our Mother

*Our Mother on the right with my aunty Kathleen
and me as flower girl. (Famly photo)*

Our mother passed so suddenly to a massive
stroke. She was so fit and healthy up until then, that
this came as a huge shock to all of us.

She died in my dad's arms. Sometimes I
think this is how it was meant to be. They were
inseparable in life maybe this is how it should be
now. As a family, we were numb with the
suddenness of it all. We all supported each other at
that time and continue to support each other now.

My mother was a lady, and this was shown in
the days following her passing by the hundreds of
people that called to my dad.
Her spirit remains and lives within all of us, her
children, and grandchildren.

I often have the feeling of hearing her speak.
Her voice was low, it was a woman's voice that had a

smooth quality to it, except when she was angry of course. Then, it could take on the sharpness that would bite into your brain. When our mother was upset, she did not hold back in letting us know. Her voice was not the only indicator, she had a look that replaced a thousand words. One look especially in church and you would stay perfectly still. Her voice and her sayings are written into my being. It was the soundtrack to my whole existence. She had two voices: one she used with us and one she used on the phone. This was her important voice.

I am losing the memory of her voice. The voice that was as familiar as my own is becoming distant. When I try to recall it now, something within me listens out and waits, quietly, as though expecting her to speak to me as she used to. Even though I stay still, her voice does not come. I will never hear it again and this saddens me.

My brother, my sisters and I can only hope we honour her spirit as it is our spirit to pass on now.

In remembering my mother I hope you will cherish the memories of your mother living or dead. Losing someone you love bores down into you like a corkscrew, but when you lose your mother, it burrows right into your very core.

It hollows you out and leaves a vacant, empty pit. Some of us try to fill this emptiness with busyness. Some of us fill it with work. Some with alcohol.
I am trying to fill it by writing this book.

At the very least I am fulfilling a lifelong dream, but I hope to honour my mother, her spirit, her church, but mostly her love of community.
It is amazing the things you find out about someone when they are gone.

Life will never be the same, but we will keep her alive forever in our hearts. I will honour her with my life. Sometimes I feel bad for laughing and I remember my mother used to say that I could be heard laughing in the next parish and that brings a smile to my face. In fact, it makes me laugh louder.

Brid Pierce grew up in Shanakyle, Parteen, County Clare. She was a middle child of a large family and was in essence a bit of a bossy boots but always a very capable woman. Our mother and father met and became what we know as a love story.

So united, so inseparable, and so respectful of each other. They both loved their family, their community, and their church. They were friendly, hospitable, honest, hardworking and they cared for others. Dad had a very good sense of humour and loved to laugh and tease our mum. She was compassionate, perhaps to a fault, but she could always stand up for herself when needed. In old pictures, when she was a child, she looked pretty and without self-importance. She was independent but worried easily when it came to her family. I remember her and her sisters mostly in the styles of the sixties. They dressed so well.

Our parents enjoyed community interaction as they were very sociable. Our mother was one of the founding members of the ICA, it was a place of bonding and a place of connection not only for the women of Broadford but for women of the surrounding areas also.

They met the first Tuesday of every month and always had a guest speaker as well as a crafts competition and a variety of skills demonstrations. The local Broadford branch of the ICA recently celebrated its fiftieth year.

Broadford ICA dinner dance 1970's

Honestly, if these women were in charge of our country, we would be in much better shape.

I recall one time mam and dad went to an ICA dinner dance both dressed up to the nines. Dad looked so handsome in his suit with his hair slicked back and mum wearing a beautiful maxi dress with her hair piled on her head in a beehive. They made such a beautiful couple, but that night they encountered a car crash on their way home, and both came back covered in blood. The community-minded couple stayed with the injured until the ambulance arrived.

Like them, I love community, I love the fact that we are connected by one or more interests. I see a community as being a common thread in a common area that brings people together to encourage and support each other.

As human beings, we all need a sense of belonging, a sense of connectedness. We got this from our parents. They instilled in us the value of friendship and to this day I have friends I met on my first day at school. It is because of them I place such value in good friendships.

I grew up thinking that everyone had a life like us but that is simply not true. Our family was a safe, loving place. We consistently felt loved.

As the eldest in the family, a fact my siblings never let me forget, I was the first to have children. My parents were my never-ending support. They were an example of how couples should love each other.

Our parents are the reason we are here, they held us up. They are the one stable anchor during our whole life, the constant.

Brid and Patrick met in the 1950s and after what seems to have been a wonderful courtship, they danced their way to marriage in 1961. They moved to London for a bit where they found work. They had a strong work ethic and a lot of hope.

To accept your parents have aged is to accept that you have too, after mum died, I was faced with the unpleasant reality of my own mortality. Of course, my brain knew that my parents would not live forever. My heart, however, had not quite caught up with that idea. In fact, it still has not because I firmly believe my father will live forever. He is fit and strong and although he misses mam like crazy, he keeps going for the rest of us. Two years on, and it still affects us all.

A piece of our life jigsaw has been detached. However much we reshuffle the other pieces, they never fit in the same way again.
My parents were perfect to my mind together they were a powerhouse. They were totally opposite and they complemented each other.

Our dad is a legend in his own lifetime. He is a shining light to us girls on how men should treat

41

us and to our brother he is a wonderful example. He continues to teach us the importance of community, connection and belonging.

When things are not going well for us, we need our community the most. Especially the community of family. We could not have gone through our mother's untimely passing without family and community.

Earlier I spoke of the large but intimate gathering for Johnny where I saw the community coming together and making a difference.

I will never, ever forget the community of Broadford when it came to our mother's funeral.

We followed tradition and ritual mostly for our father but also because it would have been what our mother wanted. Looking back now it was such a beautiful, dignified, sad but celebratory commemoration of her. Nana 'B'. The family came together like never before. Reminiscing, laughing, crying, consoling each other. She would have been so proud of all her family and especially her community. The choir coming out to sing for her would have blown her mind. I thank Broadford for that. I feel so lucky to have belonged to a culturally rich and loving community. This community along with my parents shaped my identity.

Our parents are a central stabilizing and informing force in our lives.
Between my parents, my family, and my community I developed a fascination and a major interest in the world around me.
My mind was ignited by a love for my family and deep respect and appreciation for my community. After all, what is community about, if not about caring? Community saves us from alienation and isolation.

In my parent's time, community was about finding a place we could call home. A place where we felt safe and secure. Supported in our life choices. Their generation instilled in us values and morals. They were proud good people and in coming together in their communities they characterised what was important to them. As a society, we have somewhat taken a more selfish view. We are fast becoming a 'because I'm worth it' society. We can restore balance.

In the past, our communities were shaped by religious institutions. We now know this was not always warranted.

We need to look to new leadership and to a new way of seeing things, however, remaining faithful to our roots and our foundational communities. People and their needs should be at the centre. The modern way of life is certainly challenging our ability to find balance and this cannot be good for the future of our children. We should not let our traditions and our support systems fall away.

For my mum and her generation, there were pressures, but they were always there for each other. Presently the pressure of making money and of owning 'stuff' is cutting into the quality time we have for family and friends but most of all it gives us little or no time for ourselves. Will this make us happy? I suggest not. I want to live in a world of connection, not one of disconnection.

As human beings we need connectedness and we need the lived experience of others. It is not that the past was all rosy as there was a drain of young people leaving the country. We can draw lessons from the past while dealing with the present.

Mam and Dad 1959

Mam and Dad 1960

Mam and Dad 27/09/1962

Our story of Heart

On a July day three years ago, we walked
into the church in Broadford to celebrate our
mother's life. The choir she loved so well sang and I
remember shivering, worrying about our dad and
hoping I would not botch our mother's eulogy. It was
the one thing I wanted to do for her. I wanted people
to know the woman she was. The church was
packed. My brother, sisters and children looked
empty, absent, all eyes now on us. There was no
escape from the sadness at that moment. Our pain
and fear were palpable. Our mother and our father
were stalwarts in the community and were very well
known in the surrounding locality.

I was humbled by the life Brid Pierce O'Connell had created. We can honestly say she had exactly the life she wanted. Married to the love of her life, parenting four children, belonging to a community in which she was so involved.

In dedicating this book to her and her love of community I would like to let you know where she came from. Born Bridget Pierce to mother Christina Connors-Pierce and father, Simon Pierce and was brought up in Shanakyle, Parteen, County Clare with eleven brothers and sisters. There were six boys Mike, Simon, Pat, Tom, James and John and six girls Ester (Mamie), Kathleen, Ellen, Pauline, Mags and Brid (our mother). The Pierces lived in Shanakyle since at least the 1800s and possibly longer. I hope to delve into this sometime. I do know that my paternal grandfather, my mother's father Simon was born to Michael and Bridget Pierce in 1893. As shown in the 1901 census he had two sisters, Mary and Ellie as well as two brothers, Patrick and Michael.

My maternal grandmother was Christina Connors, and she was born to James and Katie Connors Newtown, Kiltenanlea, Clonlara where she lived with her sister Maggie and brothers, Thomas, and Michael until she married.

They all lived in rural Irish communities and from hearing the stories over the years they were hard times but great times. Simon was a musician and played all over the community at house dances. Christina worked hard making sure all the children were brought up well and were properly educated. I was the first grandchild in the Pierce family and had a community of aunts and uncles who doted over me for six years until my brother Pat came along and ruined it all.

The Pierce family were, and still are, very involved in the Parteen community. This stood out at our mother's funeral as they turned up in their droves.

As Annie Dillard wrote, 'How we spend our days is, of course, how we spend our lives.' And I spent my days focused on progressing, improving myself and caring for others. When my mother passed, I began reflecting on my own life and mortality. My time is mostly concentrated on other people. I regularly ask myself 'if I learn enough new things daily?' 'Do I develop new friendships and deepen old ones?'

As I get older, my friendships are even more important to me. Before mam passed, if you asked me if community was important, I would have said yes. But if I am honest, I would not have thought about it very much. I now know family and community fill my heart. Not only is community important it is essential.

After her funeral, I got a glimpse of what community looks like.

It was all the neighbours who turned up before they were asked, it was friends who called to keep everyone company and remember our mother. Groups of people appeared to bring and make food. This is what you call a real community. There is so much unity when we need it. So much heart. This is family. This is community. This is Broadford.

I felt more connected to my home community than ever before. I always feel connected to my family and close friends, but now I felt bonded. I also felt united with the people around me. They were our cushion our safeguard to the sadness surrounding us.

In this changing world, we may have hundreds of friends on Facebook, Instagram etc, but these connections are not the ones that provide us with the social comfort we need in times of difficulty. We need human contact.

The more we depend on social media for friendships, the more we seem to let our social relationships deteriorate. We all need others to survive.

I love to feel connected, and I enjoy the company of others, but I also like my own company.

There is nothing like the solitude of a walk along a beach to clear the head. The thing that makes us happiest in life is other people. And yet other people are often the first thing to fall off our list of priorities. That is why if I feel connected to someone, I nurture that friendship.

Late one night, a friend came by, we talked about mundane things, and when she left, vanishing into a bitterly cold night, I felt more at ease than I had in a long time. I am blessed with the friends in my life.

I have one friend since I was four years old, and one since I was six.
Others entered my life at various stages. They all fill my heart. I now live in Ballina/Killaloe, and I love the community there. Refelecting on my life, I decided I would strengthen my ties with the community, and I would support my friends.

I took up writing and joined a writing group. In this writing group, I found some very gentle souls whose priorities seemed so clear that I began to reshape my own. I learned to love the power of quiet. The incentive of learning. The release and the catharsis of music as well as the liberation of solitude. I spoke more frequently to my neighbours.

I wanted them to know I was there if they needed anything.

My mothers death taught me it was time for me to put down roots and also to remain faithful to my very deep connections in Broadford.

I feel like I have found my people. New friends and old ones would be there for me. My community. I used to think that community was as simple as having friends who bring wine when things fall apart and champagne when things go well. But I now understand community is an insurance policy against life's cruelty, a kind of protection against loss and disappointment and failure.

I know my community will be here for my family if I cannot be. If I die, my family will be surrounded by people who know and love them, warts, and all. In my attempt to future-proof my life, I make every day fuller. My grandmother used to say a problem shared is a problem halved.

Our parents, grandparents and great grandparents fostered great communities, we can still enjoy those communities today If we all keep connecting with people.

The concept of community may be changing. It used to be that community came for free. It was something you were born into by virtue of family, geography, or village. Community was just there for us. If we want community now, and of course we do, we need to help develop it ourselves. Were the good old days better? I am not sure, but it feels like they were more dependable. I don't think anyone will disagree when I say there seems to be a decline in 'togetherness' as many are too busy to cultivate it.

I am a little suspicious of nostalgia. The old deep loyalty to family does not always stand and religion no longer is the central pivot of community life. The traditional social institutions our parents knew now have new and lesser meanings.

I am not claiming that things used to be better, but they were different. I am, however, an eternal optimist and I refuse to believe that humankind's best days are behind us.

It would be great if we could share resources to take care of one another like the good old days. I am not sure how people in cities experience community, but rural communities are a source of good neighbours, friends, and lovers. The village once provided all these things. Everyone had an extended family network to care for their needs. The village and family are still the main sources of belonging.

Urbanization shows little signs of stopping with most of the people in the world now living in cities. Community is no longer natural or automatic and neither is a support system for our daily identity. This means that if we want it, we need to create it. We must belong somewhere. Togetherness is where the community comes in and we need to nourish it.

Our Story of Family

In Ireland, our story has changed dramatically over the years, especially in recent times. Particularly the role of the family. In some people's minds, these changes have brought about a decline in family life. In this lovely country, we enjoy our traditions. Notably, we celebrate the tradition of the family. For instance, one parent, almost always the mother, would stay at home raise the family and look after all the domestic duties while the father would go out to work.

Many of today's adults learned their basic skills from their mother. This was how it was in my parent's time.

Dad went out to work and mum stayed home to cook, clean and take care of us kids but before he left every morning dad would bring mum a cup of tea in bed.

We would spend every evening together as family and Sundays were for the 'Sunday drive'. Our story of family was not perfect, but it was close.

The Pierce side of the family was rooted in Parteen as previously mentioned but the O'Connell side of the family was rooted in Broadford. My dad Patrick was born to Lawrence O'Connell and Mary Lyons, he had three sisters Margaret, Anna and Kitty and three brothers Michael, Lawrence and Thomas. They all lived together in Violet Hill, Broadford in the house I was brought up in. I am lucky to have known my grandparents. My grandfather was born to Michael Connell and Anastasia McNamara. They lived with their children Michael, Mary, Angela, Ellen, Lawrence, John, James, Alice, Winifred, and Anastasia.

In 1901 they lived in a Broadford that seemed like a vibrant busy place. A community where the priest was Fr John Mc Cready,
Christopher Murnane was the shopkeeper, Michael Mc Cormack the baker, Edward Barron shopkeeper, Kathleen Lynch school teacher, George McDonnell Clerk, Thomas Allen postman, John O'Keeffe shoemaker, Teresa Lynch schoolmistress, Thomas Lynch teacher, Edmond Moloney publican, Michael Connell (my great-grandfather) carpenter, James Moloney mail car driver, Catherine Ryan dressmaker, Michael Bushe shoemaker. Imagining the community as it was then, gives me goosebumps.

My grandmother Mary Lyons was born to Thomas Lyons and Margaret Kingsley, she had one brother Patrick.

Unfortunately, my great grandmother Margaret died after my grandmother was born. She then went to live with Thomas Kingsley, Patrick and Katie Larkin. They also lived in this Broadford.

Every time I drive through Broadford now I imagine the bustle of the village back in my great-grandparent's time. It makes my heart sing. Our story as a family will always be ingrained with the blood and memories of our ancestors. It would be wonderful if we could be true to their traditions. Our period of history saw many changes as everything became more fast-paced than ever before.

Changes not only occurred in how we lived, in how we ate but in the things we acquired. In recent times, however, I feel we are for one reason or another returning to some of our old traditions and values. We were beginning to lose some vital skills but now we are beginning to realise the importance of holistic living. I believe we are living in a wonderful time as our ancestors lived in theirs.

We are all part of a family, and this continues to be our greatest influence. In a survey held some years ago, 62% of people acknowledged that home and family was their biggest influence.

Family is still our first community and, therefore, our greatest form of encouragement and guidance. The shape of the family has changed and the way we understood marriage and its place in society has been revolutionised. Marriage in my grandparent's and parents' time was conventional. Any other form of family was seen as scandalous.

I am so happy to live in a time where every form of family is welcomed.

Traditionally, what we call the institute of marriage was strictly defined. It was a legal bond between a man and a woman.

In this definition, the husband was recognised as the head of the household and there was a strict division of labour. The woman was dependent on her husband for income and the man was dependent on a woman for childrearing and housekeeping. All major decisions were made by the 'boss', generally the father. The mother was seen as the emotional influencer. Sons grew up learning skills from their fathers and daughters from their mothers. The traditional roles were well defined.

The wider community was also a major influence. People identified themselves with their community and took great pride in that community. We were Broadford people through and through, we still are. The GAA were a great organisation. They nurtured community spirit and brought communities together in honour and pride. Families gathered at Mass every Sunday, and this generated a sense of belonging.

Roles are no longer defined as couples want to make up the rules themselves. There is much less social consensus on how men and women should perform their roles. Family is now seen as a more independent choice rather than a decision made because of social control.

The role of the Church and government is now more one of guidance than of control. Although the dominance of marriage is no longer the only acceptable form of family, it has been reported that most people still expect to marry at some point.

Research demonstrates that the institution of the family is our very first form of community. It is our first experience of belonging. As human beings, we all need that feeling of belonging and that feeling of connectedness.

Family values can be learned from single parents as well as the traditional mum and dad.

We must admit few families are ideal. We all have our issues. We all have our struggles. Nonetheless, we are communities of love, even if we struggle with the concept sometimes.

I feel the most important thing you can do for your family is very simple and that is to develop a strong family story. Tell a positive story about yourself and your ancestors. When faced with a challenge just add a new chapter to your story on overcoming hardship. Create and retell the story of your family's positive moments and your ability to bounce back from the difficult ones. Reconstruct the story of the community so it will thrive for many generations to come.

My O'Connell grandparents

My Pierce grandparents

Our Story of Church

When we consider the history of the Christian church through the ages, we see evidence of both goodness and sin, of kindness and cruelty, of compassion and coldness. We also see great leaps forward and devastating steps backwards. The Christian faith can be of immense reassurance and comfort especially when in times of great need. Of course, all faiths offer the same comfort but in Ireland, in the past, we were predominantly Catholic. Nonetheless, we should not become complacent or smug as we need to continue the search for truth, the search for inner peace and the search for contentment. Finding inner peace can only be a good thing for each one of us, after all, we have a two-thousand-year history to learn from.

Taking a realistic view of life and especially of the Church, we should look to some of its 2,000-year history. Christianity began with the Jewish community and thanks to the missionary passion of Paul of Tarsus, who founded Christian communities as he journeyed, a basis for Christianity was established. The first apostles who were the eyewitnesses to the life of Jesus were the interpreters of his intentions. They heard Jesus speak and they wanted others to know what he had to say. Jesus also told them to 'Go into all the world and preach the Good News to everyone'. This era became known as the apostolic age, and it saw the appearance of the New Testament.

Catholics recognise both the scriptures and the apostolic tradition as the principal guide in charting a future as a Church.

Listening to the word of God written in scripture can bring great comfort to many people. I love the parables as I feel there is a lot we can learn from them and you don't need to be religious. I love reading or re-enacting the parables with young people, they love storytelling. It is amazing the messages they take away from these ancient stories in today's modern world. After the apostolic age, thinkers and leaders continued to explore the message of Christ. These were known as our 'Church Fathers'. During the first 300 years, the Church was seen as a threat by the rulers of the day and the Christians were often persecuted and killed for their beliefs. This was most likely because Christians were seen as a threat. This began to change as Constantine who was then an emperor, became a Christian. Christianity was now an established religion and people began to recognise it as such. Groups of Christians began to take a contemplative lifestyle as a visible witness to the Gospel thus beginning the monastic movement.

This Christian monastic way of life was simple at first, but soon its everyday routine became more and more complex and diverse with each passing century. Monks and nuns could be found in the strangest of places in caves, on islands, in cemeteries, all declaring their calling to God and pronouncing their beliefs. In the end, they devised specific rules and detailed regulations. This helped them be more uniform in their expressions of Christianity in the monastic movement.

The monasteries turned out to be a vital link in the Church's survival. Europe was flourishing as a Christian community, but it suffered devastating foreign invasions which threatened to destroy its civilizations. The established monasteries, however, managed to help the Church to rise.

The years 700-1300 saw the growth of a western Christian community where new schools and universities came into existence, nurturing a rich development in philosophy and theology. They had their challenges even then as there was a growing division between the Church in the East and the Church in the West over theological points of difference. This was a difficult time in the history of the Church. Hope was restored with people like Francis of Assisi who founded the Franciscans. They showed witness on how to live life without violence and force. Maybe Pope Francis will bring positivity.

During the fourteenth century, a strong movement of disapproval from within the Church began to quarrel against the hierarchy and the papacy. Back then there was a refusal by the authorities to recognise the need for renewal. Does this remind us of anything? Are authorities still not recognising the need for renewal? It was then that many like Martin Luther gave up hope. They broke away, establishing their own Church. This was a tragic chapter in history.

The Roman Catholic Church remained in union with the Pope. Seeking to reaffirm its foundational beliefs, the Council of Trent was called (1545-63). A new world missionary period was born. Christian missionaries began to travel bringing the Catholic faith far and wide. They were received with a mixture of emotions, but they persisted in their belief that they were bringing the good news.

As we move on to the eighteenth century, we find new intellectual forces of secularization. This became known as the Enlightenment. Western ways of thinking became more and more at odds with religion and the Church. The Church was in a period of struggle.

The introduction of Christianity to us here in Ireland dates to sometime around the year 400AD. Monasteries were dotted around the country for those who wanted peace and tranquillity. Monastic schools in Ireland became centres of excellence for people all over Europe. Secular subjects were taught but there was a very strong emphasis on scripture and religious studies. These monasteries served as a refuge and haven to many great scholars and theologians.

Great manuscripts were produced, one of these being The Book of Kells which can still be viewed at Trinity College, Dublin. There was a major threat to our monasteries and churches during the ninth and tenth centuries as Vikings reached the Irish shores and they began pillaging. After the Viking invasion, the English began trying to take control of the Irish under Henry III. It was not until the seventeenth century that the Crown of England gained full control of Ireland. Ireland was progressively colonised, nonetheless, the majority of Irish people remained Roman Catholic.

By the late eighteenth century, many of the Anglo-Irish had come to see Ireland as their native country. It was a difficult time for Catholics as they could not enter parliament or become government officials. In 1728, the Catholics outnumbered Protestants five to one. A few Catholics managed to hold their estates with the collaboration of friendly Protestants. If we fast forward to 1922 with the partition of Ireland, 92.6% of the population were Catholic. Through all their persecution the people of Ireland remained steadfast in their faith. When priests were not allowed to celebrate Mass during penal times, they and worshippers had to find hidden areas in the countryside to celebrate Mass.

Many of these places were marked with "Mass Rocks".

The Mass Rock was sometimes taken from a church ruin and used as a place of worship. Almost every community in Ireland boasts its own Mass rock. There was one in Broadford I visited often as a child. It was spine-chilling to stand where my ancestors stood many years before. I often imagined how this felt for them and the trouble to which they went to worship. Most Mass rocks are very difficult to locate, but in our youth, my friends and I were very inquisitive, and we liked to ramble around our locality looking for different places and local well know landmarks. Like St. Peter, an eighteenth-century carving on the church wall, to whom people told their secrets. Rumour had it he relieved all worries. If St Peter ever speaks, we will all be in trouble.

It often gave us an eerie feeling to stand where people had stood in the past during times of oppression. We often tried to imagine what life must have been like for them all those years ago. Our ancestors were very brave people. Catholicism formed their backbone and the backbone of Irish society. Tension throughout the religious world continued into the twentieth century. This provided a push that led to the calling of a meeting of bishops from all over the world. This was called the Second Vatican Council and was a watershed time for the Church. It took place between 1963 and 1965. Vatican II brought a fresh perspective to all interested parties. A fresh perspective was brought to bear upon all facets of Church life. It presented a vision of 'the people of God' as Church rather than the hierarchical dimension.

It brought about remarkable changes. The Mass was said in the language of the people rather than in Latin and lay initiatives were fostered which remain a feature of the Church to this day. These initiatives will be needed even more into the future if the Church hopes to survive.

St Peters Church Broadford
Photo Niamh Quinn

Chapter Two

Hope: Past, Present and Future

"Nothing should be out of the reach of hope. Life
is a hope."
Oscar Wilde

Eighteenth Century Carving of St Peter,
Photo by Niamh Quin

Looking Back

Growing up in a small rural village in County Clare was a joy for me. Looking back now I have many standout memories. I remember the Church being a central focus of daily life as it was for everyone back then. I lived with my parents and grandparents, as was the norm in those days, and though I am sure it was not ideal for my parents, it was magic for a little girl to live with so many people who loved her. That is until my brother came along when I was six, sorry Pat you know I love you! My younger sisters Claire and Clodagh came along after my grandparents died.

My grandparents are ever-present in my life and even to this day, I still dream about them. They had a major influence on me. At the time I did not appreciate the rituals and traditions to which they exposed me. I felt they were an interruption to my otherwise playful life. I remember kneeling down to pray the rosary each night, this was torture to me as a young child. My mind would be anywhere but on the prayer. I remember we would always say a prayer in the morning and before meals. We were not the Waltons, although my dad and granddad had a sawmill. We had our traditions and rituals which were of huge importance to our family life. This is something I now appreciate.

Our little rural village was the centre of our universe. Family and neighbours were everything. Yes, they were often talked about and given out about, nevertheless, they were prayed for and appreciated. Community and Church were all tied into one. We had a parish priest and a curate, who were all-seeing, all-knowing.

I remember many priests in my time in Broadford but there was one standout one for me. He was very progressive for the time. His name was Fr Pat Sexton and he taught us all to take pride in our pretty little village. He gathered people together in different townlands, we planted flower gardens and took pride in our area. In Violet Hill where I lived, we put in a picnic table with lawn and flower bushes it was a joy to sit there on a sunny day with my friends. We seemed to have so many more sunny days then. This area is still there today.

Fr Sexton also founded the youth club with some dedicated members of the parish, and this was a fantastic outlet for us young teens at the time. Community then seemed simple; it revolved around the Church, the school, the parish hall and the GAA. Mass was only celebrated on a Sunday. When Saturday night Mass was introduced, people thought that will never work, insisting that 'Sunday is not Sunday without Mass'. Times have changed since then. My foundation, my inner being, my belief system is in Catholicism. That is not to say that I have always followed its doctrine. I have tried to live a good life. I attribute that to my parents and grandparents. Remembering the ritual of the rosary does not fill me with joy but the time spent together as a family gave me a good moral grounding.

I admit I no longer say the rosary, but I do sit with myself and reflect each night. I have a great ability to dream, something I often got myself in trouble for at school. But I see it as a positive. I am always looking to the future and imagining something better. We all long for the good old days but were they really that good? I remember my youth fondly here, but I would not go back. They were hard times. They were unquestioning times and I like to question.

As children we were expected to speak when spoken to and obey the rules. Especially the rules of the church. At that time boys were serving mass I questioned why I could not serve and was told it is not for girls. It was not polite to question the parish priest.

My parents together with my grandparents gave me great grounding but now it is up to me. In the same vein, our ancestors gave us all a significant foundation and now it is down to us to build on this. My Grandmother gave me a Bible, a white leather-bound heavy volume which was her pride and joy. I still have this Bible. I opened it today randomly and there in front of me was Proverbs 29:18 'Where there is no vision, the people will perish.' We need vision in every area of our life or indeed we will perish. There are many people out there who would like to return to the past. But we cannot go back even if we wanted to. For growth, we need to move forward.

Too many of us have a limited way of thinking. We are happy to settle for the way things have been done. It is time for us to dream. To re-imagine. To become a people of opportunities. A people of possibilities. Our history is not without fault. Our future will not be without fault, but we must not disengage. We need to figure out where to go from here. Religious beliefs and practices have been a worldwide feature of society. People prayed, worshipped, and sacrificed. They were also deep thinkers with the result they have evolved and developed the communities we now have.

The Catholic Church in Ireland is experiencing challenging times right now but not for the first time. In the eighteenth century during the Penal Laws in Ireland, the Catholic Church was oppressed as the English crown tried to browbeat people from practising their religion.

Rituals and ceremonies involving Catholic clergy were forbidden. Many churches were destroyed, and others were put to use by the Protestant Church. Nevertheless, the Irish people remained faithful to the celebration of the Mass and two new traditions came into being. Those were the Mass Rock and the Station Mass. To celebrate Mass at the Mass Rock Catholics gathered at a spot marked by a rock usually in the countryside and in a secluded place. Often the priest would arrive in disguise. He placed the sacred vessels on the rock while designated locals would keep a lookout. They would choose vantage points in the landscape where they could see any English militia approaching. They are still deemed to be special, sacred places.

The other option for Mass was to hold it in people's homes. The word was put about locally that Mass was to be said in a specific house on a particular day. The neighbours would gather for what might be the only opportunity to get Mass for some time. This was a difficult time, and it was not safe for the priest to carry sacred vessels or vestments. He would leave these in the care of the local community. The locals called these the "Mass kit" and they were passed from house to house as they were needed. These Masses turned into what we now call 'the Station Mass'. Little by little during the first half of the nineteenth century things improved and churches were built across the countryside to replace the Mass houses. We could learn a lot from how our ancestors overcame adversity.

With the passing of Catholic Emancipation in 1829, Catholics were free to worship openly. When each community built its own church, the tradition of the Station Mass was kept alive. It was a special occasion to welcome the neighbours.

Mass was usually followed by food and chat, with singing and music if you were lucky. This Mass was preceded by weeks of preparation. It was a time to show the house off at its best. There would be painting, wall-papering, cleaning, shopping and cooking. The social changes of recent decades mean that the Station Mass has disappeared. I believe there is a version of the Station Mass happening in some local communities.

Perhaps we could take aspects of the tradition around the Station Mass and maybe have a spiritual or reflective evening in our homes. It would be wonderful to take time out with neighbours. There is a parish near me, Sixmilebridge, where they choose a farm, a local Mass Rock or lake shore and each year they hold what could be described as a communal Station Mass. This has proven to be a success and is a fantastic way for all the community to come together and connect. It is an excellent way of promoting inclusion.

We could all take ideas from this tradition. The pattern of what happens could be varied to suit each locality. I suspect it would work best at the local level. It would be wonderful to spend time together in a social, peaceful, tranquil and fun atmosphere. Even in this changing Ireland of challenging times, it could be a real and profound occasion for the local community to extend the hand of welcome to new neighbours. Perhaps a special effort to personally contact each neighbour to invite them would be looked on favourably. I know from experience people like to be personally invited. It shows appreciation and respect. I believe people deserve the personal touch. However, it is also important to put out an open invitation. Everyone is welcome at the table.

Our past informed our present so maybe now we can look back again with a view to our future. Working out how to move forward acknowledging where we are. Recognise the challenges, get creative, and meet people where they are even if that is in their townland.

Learning from the Past

Maturity brings with it wisdom, tolerance and understanding. It is hoped that we learn from our past mistakes, even as we wrestle with new ones. In communities, we underwent a maturing process. Hopefully, we can look to our past, reflect on our mistakes and what we got right. We inherit our strengths and weaknesses from our ancestors so hopefully as we mature, we will find what it is to be human and live our best life. As I matured, I began to see rules differently. I saw them as guidelines that had been handed down through the generations and were of great value. I learned the value of tradition. We are so lucky to have such wonderful traditions. What I thought was old fashioned during my youth I now understand to be wonderful rituals and customs. We should embrace these rituals and customs. Adapt and modify them to suit our present times.

I lived in a time that was exciting when there were cries across the world to 'make love not war'. There was a hunger for peace. There was an appetite for happiness. We think of ourselves as a people deeply immersed in tradition. This self-image is shown in our literature, our plays, our storytelling, and our folklore. Our mentality has remained strong despite the attempts of oppression. I feel confident that I was born at a great time in history.

A time of questioning. A time of searching. A time of seeking. A time in pursuit of understanding. We should move forward remembering the past and building on valuable tradition.

There is no way to recover the past, even if we wanted to. We should make new traditions. In the past, the present and the future, there is one constant and that is love. In this vast universe of ours, each one of us relates to love in his or her own way. It is a very personal thing. Faith is also a very personal thing. Love and faith permeate our world and our community. It is up to us to realise our full potential. By living with love and compassion we can build sustainable communities into the future. Unless our society engages with reality, we risk losing our sense of tradition and community. Some form of healing is required, recognising love as a way forward. Growing up in Ireland is a privilege. It may have been tough at times, but the sense of community was always there, even though we drift from time to time we look to our community for support.

The Second Vatican Council endorsed the good news that the church was called to be the 'light of the world'. The publication of these documents shared all human hopes and fears. The mood was optimistic, positive even ecstatic. It would be great if we could harness that mood again. While change occurred for a time, it lapsed. Hopefully, now we will be able to find those feelings again.

In our past, a hierarchy was how the Church rolled and although it is packaged differently it still rolls that way. At present, it is in poor shape but if it takes up the challenges presented to it and addresses them now, it may have a chance of being relevant in some form.

As Churches are big and empty a great part of the time, maybe we can be creative and look to utilising them differently. As communities, we need to ask the questions no matter how difficult. What is at the heart of our community and how will we save it? The church may have gained more power in Ireland than it did in other countries, but the power was accepted. It was intertwined with our state laws. It is difficult to believe now, but it was only in 1977 that legislation was passed stopping unmarried women from losing their job if they became pregnant. It was ten years later before the concept of illegitimacy was abolished. These are not just concerns of the past, they inform our present and they should help us shape our future.

In developing true compassion, we can embrace a new future where Church and community can flourish for all its members. This means remembering that Church is not the building but is, in fact, all the people. Giving these people a greater voice can only benefit all involved. Looking back can sometimes help us look forward.

Give a damn about the past

I acted in several Brian Friel plays and I love the insight he has into Irish society. In Philadelphia Here I Come he looked for 'a vast restless place that doesn't give a damn about the past!' We all long for that at times but we cannot deny our past. Wherever we travel in the world we look for a little bit of Ireland. Admit it, if you go on holiday there is always that one thing you cannot do without. For me, it is Taytos while for others it may be teabags, butter or potatoes.

We all want to experience a little bit of home when we are in less familiar environments. This begs the question, are we capable of living in the present or are we stuck in the past. We sometimes find ourselves looking back musing about times that maybe never happened. Our memories are rose-tinted. We are very good at creating a fictional pastoral paradise. We should celebrate our Irish culture, but should we remain stuck? We should be proud of our Irish culture and our traditions, but should we be slaves to them. I believe not. I love being Irish, I love our culture and our traditions, but I also enjoy new experiences. It is good to look back to see how we arrived where we are. But we should do so honestly and truthfully.

Looking back nostalgically at our past may affect how we live our present and prevent us from moving forward. As Ireland remembered the 1916 Centenary, society began looking at itself and its identity. As a woman, I began thinking of my cultural value. I, and women I know, have continuously highlighted what we see as continued patriarchal discrimination within Ireland. Over the past fifty years we have seen major change but is it enough? The role of women in society has been one of the greatest changes. Women are now participating in the workforce to a greater extent. They began taking on professional positions and this has caused a shift in the family dynamic.

Family has always been and continues to be important to Irish society and although the societal beliefs surrounding women in the family have changed over time, perhaps parallel changes have not taken place for the supposed roles of men. For my mother's generation and indeed for my own, women had to juggle their careers, while still taking on the lion's share of the housework.

Lives have changed since my younger days. We are now expected to work harder and longer than ever before. Times have changed so much since I began working, I am happy to say that life will be very different for my children. I often think if my grandparents were to return today what would they think? I suspect they would barely recognise where they came from. Certainly, the family structure has radically changed. The traditional family, the married couple with children all living in the same house has changed and is continuing to change. I saw it written that one-in-three families in Ireland are moving away from this so-called 'traditional model.' Our modern society is now home to more unconventional families. Families like cohabiting couples, lone parents, divorced or separated parents.

People are choosing to get married at different times. How they marry is also changing with many opting for a registry office or hotel wedding with a celebrant in place of a priest. Couples getting married seem to be more equal. However, they are faced with negotiating household chores, finance, and if they have children, who will be the one to go out to work and who will stay home? There is more choice but with this, comes more stress. In the past couples tended to work things out, stay together and keep the traditional family intact. Now with the increased acceptance of divorce, the traditional face of the family is changing.

Our communities are transforming. We are new thinking communities embracing diversity. The increasing diversity within our family dynamics will inspire and influence all kinds of interactions. Communities who embrace them will enjoy cultural and ethnic differences for the betterment of all. At a conference in Mary Immaculate College Limerick in July 2017, Cardinal Christoph Schönborn addressed a conference on 'Let's Talk Family: Let's Be Family.' Schönborn, a son of a divorced couple, advocated for more 'merciful' communities, especially towards divorcees and same-sex couples. He advised that some marriages cannot last forever and 'dramas happen in life; That's life.' Be more compassionate, more tolerant and everyone will benefit. From ancient times Irish culture was formed around kinship groups or clans. In modern times the clannishness remains. For many, the family is considered the centre of personal relationships that create identity, unity, and security. Family cohesion is central to the traditional Irish family culture.

Our Present Reality

In Ireland, at this present time, all our churches are in crisis. The congregations and clergy are ageing. Where the Catholic Church is concerned, a recent MRBI poll found that the number of Catholic priests in Ireland dropped forty-three per cent in the twenty years to 2015. Numbering 2,019, their average age is approaching sixty-five. Just eighty are studying for the Catholic priesthood compared to 526 in 1990.

People's loyalty is fluctuating. They mainly attend on special occasions or to mark significant rites of passage, but they describe themselves as Catholics. Tradition and ritual are still important. Maybe we are reverting to early nineteenth-century patterns of devotion when both clergy and churches were smaller in number.

Throughout the centuries there has always been an ebb and flow of religious practice. The Catholic Church at present is at a low ebb as it looks to the future with great unease.

The decreasing numbers of priests mean that clergy simply cannot be present in the way they were in the past. The Church was always seen as the centre of the community this may have to change. Initiatives are being introduced in various diocese throughout the country where liturgies are lay-led. Allocating people to lead parishes may be a way of ensuring Churches exist locally. This is being met with resistance. Throughout my travels, I found that the local Church is central to local communities. Although life is moving fast away from what we knew as children, it is still faithful to many of our rituals and traditions.

The future of the community in Ireland is likely to be very different. The lack of priests will be severely felt in the coming years. A new model of the community will hopefully emerge. The parish priest is not accountable for everything that happens in the community. Every member has their own gifts and talents to offer. Laity is becoming more involved, but there is a barrier that the Church and community still belong to clergy and the religious. In my experience, this barrier comes as much from the laity as clergy.

The preconditioning of the past is very difficult to shift. The clergy have seen the writing on the wall for some time as they were aware of the dwindling number entering seminaries. The laity, however, was not privy to this information. It is easy to ignore what is happening until it affects your community.

In my community, there was consternation recently, when there was great difficulty in getting a priest for a local woman's death. The local parish priest was away, the neighbouring priest had fallen ill.

There was a search for other neighbouring priests to attend the funeral but they each had their own prior commitments. It took six phone calls before a priest already under severe pressure made himself available to the family. We are all happy to go along with our business until we are faced with a situation like this. Who will be there for our dead?

It brings it home to us the changes that are occurring. We can give out about 'the lack of priests', we can say 'the bishops are the problem' or 'I'm sick of it all' until we need one of the sacraments. Lay involvement in parish and community life is now being strongly promoted. Pope Benedict's message was clear. He said the church needs 'a mature and committed laity, able to make its specific contribution to the mission of the church.' 'Lumen Gentium' one of the principal documents of Vatican II, puts it best when it describes the style of relationships within the church as, 'familial.' Considering the church as a family highlights a shared responsibility. Pastoral Councils looked at what it means to be Church. They agreed the Church is all the people and all the people should be welcome to participate.

Pastoral Councils and community members want to see steps taken. They are tired of talking shops and deeper thinking and feel abandoned. This is true, especially for women. They are the majority in the pews, but they are few when it comes to decision making. Some sincere good men and women have no problem speaking about their own spirituality. They understand and recognise that all mission does not lie with clergy. They know it is their calling and it requires a self-understanding that is theological at its core. It would be great if the narrowmindedness of the culture of clericalism was abolished.

Clericalism may have worked in the past, but it will not work into the future. The trust the Irish people had is deeply damaged.

It will be very difficult to regain confidence. Most priests, however, have outstanding support and are highly regarded by their community. If the Church is to be relevant in today's world it needs to have a worthwhile message and be more open in its approach.

Building Hope

These past years have been tough in Catholic Ireland 'the island of saints and scholars.' Working within the realms of the inner sanctum of the Catholic Church opened my eyes to the challenges and difficulties it faced. It certainly was not the Church I was exposed to as a child. In many ways, it has been a time of calamity. The abuse scandals were beyond heartbreak, but the cover-up was even more hurtful. There is no excuse, never was and never will be for the behaviour of the people involved. The lives of so many people have been irrevocably harmed and the effects have been far-reaching. Morale has never been so low.

Working across the Diocese of Killaloe was an experience I will never forget. It was a major learning experience. I met the most amazing people and encountered a genuine concern for community. It became evident very quickly that there is a need for change. People were mindful of the hurt in their communities.

It became obvious there was a need to redefine community. When a crisis happens, it forces us into sudden change. There is little or no time for thoughtful planning and decision-making.

This crisis is happening, and we are in a time of frustration and conflict. A response from leaders seems to be very slow in coming.

I was delighted to be working with the Diocese of Killaloe where questions were being asked and answers were being sought. I got the feeling this was a Diocese in transition. This transition is slow and there is resistance. Nonetheless, there are many there with vision. At least the difficulties are now being named and there is an acknowledgement that things are not quite the way they are supposed to be. Difficult times are a normal part of community life. When these times are eventually modelled by our leaders, we can begin to work through the struggles. We may learn that difficult times will be times of immense growth. Times of progress. Without doubt, the right leader can facilitate that growth through careful collaboration with all involved.

Experiencing challenges leaves us feeling a variety of deep emotions. We feel at sea. We become anxious and lack creative energy. In a time of crisis, it would be good for us to come together to comfort each other. It would be good for us to talk, to dream, to have a vision and above all to listen.

The greatest possible outcome for the Catholic Church in modern history is that of the Papal inauguration of Pope Francis. He is a great example to us all. He listens and he models the way. I have great admiration for the man. He leads by example, and this is what Jesus did.

The Church will change. It must change. It has changed many times over the past 2,000 years, however, the question is 'how should it change to serve in the twenty-first century? Pope Francis has a vision of involving everyone. Clergy alone do not hold responsibility for all the mission and all the pastoral activities of our community.

We have a responsibility to each other. Our priest cannot be everything to everyone, all the time. In my youth, we had at least two priests in every parish. Some parishes even had three. They were able to achieve more. We got accustomed to our priests always being there. A priest told me recently that when he was ordained in the 1960s he had to work in another diocese while he waited for an opening in the Diocese of Killaloe as they had over and above the number they needed. In many areas at present, there is one priest to several parishes.

Our clergy are not getting any younger, they need help. They need help from the laity. We should be empowering ourselves to be leaders and most importantly the clergy need to allow this to happen. Pope Francis both in his person and in his teachings is bringing a new source of energy and momentum to the Church. He realises that most people live in the day-to-day struggle of striving to be good.

I know when I mention Church here you will think I am talking of the Pope, the Bishops, and the Priests, and yes of course they are all essential elements to the church, but we need to realise that it is much, much, more than that. In fact, the church is the people, the church is the community, we are all the church bringing life to the world, in our relationships, in our society, in our sorrows and our joys.

Through the years I have questioned my faith and my beliefs but the one belief I have continuously held is that of the example of Jesus. I believe in how He lived and in His humanity. If we all live our lives in love as Jesus did, the world would be a much better place. I was lucky to do a degree in Theology.

But we do not need to know or understand theology to transform our communities into communities that touch lives and changes hearts, 'theology is meant to be lived not talked about'.

When I began working with the Diocese of Killaloe, it was in the throes of a listening process. A process that took place across the Diocese asking questions and listening. After this process, a Pastoral Plan, Builders of Hope, was born. This is what we all need to do, 'build hope'. Hope in our lives. Hope in our homes. Hope in our communities. Hope for our future.

Two thousand years ago a small group of people began what was to capture the whole of the Western world. They were thought then to be of no consequence. They were few and seemed to be talking rubbish. They were following a crazy man who went from town-to-town preaching. This small group of people were the first Christians. Maybe small groups of people getting together could make a difference again. They could bring love and compassion into community. It is not all about religion. It is about building togetherness for the good of all.

Building hope is not easy. It is not easy to be a Catholic in Ireland today and most especially it is not easy being a priest. The number of priests is dwindling. Priests are under constant pressure. They must respond to the day-to-day demands of their ministry being there for their community. With one priest now responsible for many parishes, they are in demand.

Those priests ministering in Ireland are left with little time to perform their regular ministries and they are now being asked to embrace change. Priests are ready to welcome change, but they are nervous about what it might bring.

There is a willingness to change but the stresses of keeping everything going can be exhausting. We cannot rely on our clergy to provide leadership anymore. We should look to what we can do to keep our communities vibrant into the future. Many people think that the changes taking place are very sudden, however, they have been persistently changing for some time. Our present reality is there is no longer a place to hide.

The Catholic Church is set to become a minority Church. The challenge is to keep our communities alive. We need to stay connected. Keep hope alive. While working with the Diocese of Killaloe we tried hard to ignite change. Despite all the efforts of those involved it is very difficult to bring everyone along. Change can be painful. Routine is comforting. Much of the leadership will come through with men and women working in communities alongside priests. They will bring enthusiasm, a new expertise and skill set which can only benefit the connectedness of all. These people will bring a lived experience to the community and a commitment of openness and welcome. A lived experience only they can bring. People working alongside each other each living out their potential is an exciting way of building hope.

Facing the future

As someone who has lived in rural Ireland all my life, I believe passionately in its people and its potential. Rural Ireland is simply beautiful. It makes a major contribution to our society. The small tight-knit communities with their natural landscape, their historical background and above all their passionate people are unique. These communities should be cherished and valued.

There are challenges to be faced, our narrative has varied throughout history, but we have never lost our identity. We are vibrant and creative.

We have faced adversity in the past and will continue to do so in the future. To maintain our way of living in our communities, we need to provide support and empower its people into the future. Cultivating our creativity and enriching our culture will contribute to the vitality of our rural areas. Supporting our people will add to the well-being of all.

As Irish people, we have many characteristics that differentiate us. We have our language, our songs, our poetry, our customs, and our games.

We have the best communities with a spirit that will never be found elsewhere. Unfortunately, since the economic downturn, rural communities have been somewhat battered. People had to move to survive, thus robbing their community of their gifts, talents, and skills.

As we transition from economy to economy, it would be great if we could find an approach that will sustain us into the future. We need a holistic approach, working together to make things better. We see the limitation of individual pursuits that have increased in recent years. The importance of connectedness and coming together to meet our needs and solve problems is coming to the fore. People can still make big changes in their community when they have the right tools.

The greatest social problem facing community life in the future is loneliness. Many are beginning to feel alienated, left behind, lonely, and depressed.

This is particularly true of people who live alone with no supports in place. One of the chief things in our life is the people we do life with. Sometimes we get so wrapped up in ourselves, feeling that we can do it all alone. So many things take up our time and energy, we do not leave enough time for relationships and the community.

With our traditional Church on the decline, community supports will be vital. We need community because it allows us to interact with each other. We can have shared experiences with like-minded people. It gives us the chance to foster valued relationships that can last a lifetime. We are living such busy lives it is difficult to become active members of our communities. If we do not participate in our communities, we will live detached, lonely lives with minimum or no contact from people outside the family circle. This is not healthy. Even though family is the most important element of our lives, it is vital to our development to get to know new people.

This is essential to our progression. Peter Block, the author of *Community: The Structure of Belonging*, said that 'functional communities help maintain a good and progressive society'. Community provides the supports we need to handle the issues of everyday lives.

It can provide the support needed to help the vulnerable in our society. Being part of a healthy community is fundamental to the development of all.

I remember growing up in Broadford we had things going on each night of the week. Dancing, music, drama, sport. There was a connectedness, a gathering. All these events would not have existed without the help of community leadership.

Having all these amenities available helped my friends and me develop into well-rounded individuals. Through these activities, we met and developed friendships with some of the best people. Indeed, most of us are still friends. A helpful, positive community improves the abilities and skills of those living there. It is important for people to feel connected to one another.

We are mutually dependent on each other for many reasons. When members of a community come together, they will motivate each other. In sharing interests and resources, they will provide much-needed support. In the past, the Church was the community hub. It was the glue that kept everything together. It is important to keep our communities active. Remembering the past is a must when we look to face the future. As we drink from a common well. Examining how we appreciate tradition and how we gather are all keys to looking to the future.

Future of Church

What can we say about the future of the Catholic Church in Ireland? There are many opinions about where it is going. They fall into three categories, those who want to return to the past, those who are in denial and say it will see them out, and those who want reform. During my time with the diocese of Killaloe, I shared responsibility for pastoral leadership. It was hoped to guide a path of renewal while implementing the pastoral plan. There were nights when we met with parishes who were optimistic. This was encouraging. Then there were nights when we were disheartened by the tired-out volunteers. They were weary from years of volunteering with no clear path.

The future of the Catholic Church in Ireland will be very different. This can only be a good thing. Renewal will come from everyone. A new way of existing. Maybe more could be offered in terms of outreach, bringing us into a deeper understanding of connection and togetherness. This could include living again our Irish traditions.

We could put pastoral programmes in place, providing healing to those who found the Church to be egotistical, listening to all the voices, and appreciating volunteers would be a good start. Throughout my life, I encountered great priests. The question is, will we have great priests into the future to assist in our communities.

Vocations are not only for priests. Many may enjoy the priesthood of the ordinary and are already natural leaders. Living their lives in love as there is so much goodness to share. Nonetheless, some withdraw from any form of responsibility. If communities are more open and welcoming, people may be more willing to participate. Eliminating the culture of clericalism may be a start. I remember a time when the clergy ruled. There are still some who are hanging on to what they feel is their domain. However, many are ready for change. Pastoral initiatives may help with this. Draw from the experience of all in the community.

In the past, the Church created and established many facilities and services within the community. Maybe communities could look to providing further services to the poor, the sick, the bereaved and the vulnerable. Perhaps we could look to providing training that can be prophetic and visionary.

Becoming the hub of ongoing formation will help bring our community forward into the future.

Right now, there is grief, and grief can take many forms. Together we can come to terms with the past and move forward to more open diverse communities. People are searching for something. There is a renewed interest in spirituality. Maybe the community could look to feeding this spiritual hunger by bringing spirituality to the heart of communities.

There is true goodness in all our communities giving them a focal point would be highly beneficial.

Pope Paul VI in 1946 called Ireland, 'the most Catholic country in the world.' That was then and this is now. Our communities can find their place in a modern society without compromising their mission. There is always hope, as Martin Luther once said 'if the world was ending tomorrow, I would still plant my apple tree today'. Maybe we need to start planting. Plant with the seeds of humility, love, compassion, and hope. The future of community in Ireland no longer lies solely with the local priest but with lay people participating, and the energy in the community. It will have more reduced numbers, but they will be people who know what it is to be compassionate leaders and are happy to sign up for all it entails. It will be a more community-led Church, a more diverse Church, and a more inclusive Church.

Moving forward

Meeting with Pastoral councils brought with it a certain energy. It was through this energy that suggestions were mooted on how local communities could be supported going forward. Moving from maintenance to mission could be the foundation.

So many know how to maintain the structures of the community. They know how to fix a roof or build a wall but so many are ignorant of their mission.

Pastoral councils saw their mission as one of outreach. This is a challenge. The purpose of each local community is to reach those who feel left out and vulnerable. Help them to feel included and take an active part in the community.

Without exception, each Pastoral Council felt their local community needed to be more inclusive. Another concept put forward was improving the Mass experience. There was a perceived need to mobilise committed parishioners to help out. There was huge frustration around this plan as those involved in Pastoral Councils had been involved for many years and could not step back. There was no one to take their place, no one to help out. So when the suggestion to get more people involved was put forward it was met with massive sighs of exasperation. 'Where are we going to get these?

Many talented people are living in communities who will not put themselves forward but will be happy to take part if asked. During the implementation of the Builders of Hope plan in the Diocese of Killaloe, it was obvious people were tired, but they were willing to try something new if it was recognised by others. Appreciation for participants in Parish Pastoral Councils is sadly scarce.

Without these committed people communities could not survive. It is so important to acknowledge the work committed volunteers do. Also, we should take inspiration from those teams already set up, parking teams, welcome teams, information teams, cafe teams, hospitably teams, bereavement teams, funeral teams, prayer teams, ministry of the word teams, ministry of the Eucharist teams, church flower teams, church cleaners and more. A major question always asked is how do we mobilise the next generation? The big question is continuously on youth. How do we get youth involved?

Sadly, there is no definitive answer to this question, other than it is unlikely we will get our youth back into the church. But by harnessing their gifts, talents, and enthusiasm the community will benefit.

For instance, weekend programmes for children that stand alongside Mass would be a great way of prodding their interest. Make it fun and interactive, not babysitting but pray and play where they hear readings, sing songs, and listen to parables through creative measures. Programmes that include fun, with adult ministers available to interact. I experienced a greater involvement, greater energy, and a prayerful atmosphere in the churches where play and prayer were available to the community.

To keep youth involved maybe we could explore starting small groups. Examine moral-centred friendships. Young people love to learn through stories. Maybe having weekly small groups in a parish is the way forward for the communities of the future. Reaching out to our young is needed, it is my experience that young people have deep goodness.

They look after each other, show a healthy interest in justice and peace as well as the integrity of creation. We as adults should be providing them with opportunities to express these interests.

'The Church really needs to change': how many times do we hear this? Every time I meet a group, they speak of the Church changing, the people are the Church, so let us ask the question, are the people willing to change?

If communities are to experience change, baby steps and patience are required.

Change will come slowly, but it will be worth it to have inclusive, nourishing communities. Communities, we are proud to pass on to those who follow, pass on solid traditions like our ancestors did for us. Today's generation is struggling. One of the greatest problems is lack of focus and poor self-esteem.

One of the best ways of fostering self-esteem is to encourage young people, give them a space to use their talents, allow them the opportunity to give.

It is good for all of us to give of ourselves, of our time and our talents. To be of value to others through giving improves confidence and self-respect. In proactively seeking to live out our lives to the fullest we learn to value ourselves, our community, and those who live there. This can only be positive. It has been said that we live in a culture of compromise, deception, materialism, and appearance. This culture has left people searching for something. Perhaps that is something to support. By igniting hearts and minds, especially the hearts and minds of young people, a new enthusiasm is born. We need a sense of passion.

There is a hunger out there. This is a hunger for reaching fulfilment. It is a hunger to find spirituality. If we look to the example of our forefathers, we will find the courage to make the change we so desperately seek. A young person once said to me 'that is all very well but I don't believe in God'. I asked him 'did he believe in Jesus'. He said 'I believe there was a man called Jesus who did good things'. 'Well then' I said, 'why not start there learn from the life lessons Jesus taught us, do good things and you are sure to live a better if not fulfilled life?'. Maybe in time, this young man will find his God.

We are all obsessed with immediacy, finding that fulfilment, that spirituality right now.

Being guided by the example of our ancestors will help us to recognise the best version of ourselves. It will teach us to participate in our communities, find work uniquely suited to us and help us engage in our social responsibilities. In doing this, we may find fulfilment.

Evangelisation is another way we can help change. Mentioning this word at Pastoral Council meetings made people feel very uncomfortable. Maybe because people had the image of standing in market squares and shouting out their beliefs to all and any who would listen? Or maybe it reminds us of Evangelical churches where their methods are intimidating and argumentative? Or perhaps it reminds us of television evangelists who have been linked with any number of scandals over the years? Evangelisation, however, means sharing our good deeds with the whole world.

There are many ways of doing this. Showing a good example in our communities and encouraging even challenging others to do the same is evangelisation. It should be our purpose to influence communities by bringing positivity to every corner of that community. Be contagious. Make positivity infectious. Encourage everyone to use their talents for the good of all the community.

Everyone benefits from this, the receiver, and the giver. Above all do this in love and compassion, not with rumourmongering and gossip. Gossip is one of the most damaging elements to any community. Sometimes we cannot help ourselves, but we should resist the temptation to take part in tittle-tattle and hearsay. People's reputations can be ruined by this and the community can be damaged irrevocably.

We need to eliminate our narrowmindedness, our judgemental biases and open our hearts to the possibilities of the future. Our communities are full of people living caring lives. They are living out their calling.

We are a nation of storytellers. The telling of our story as community is a terrific way of inspiring and encouraging change into the future. Stories can change people's lives.

The stories of Francis of Assisi, St Bridget, Pope Francis influenced my life. The stories of many ordinary people I met throughout my life have also greatly benefited me.

We all have a story and sharing this with others can be motivating to them. We all have faults and failings, but our journey can be empowering to those around us. While speaking with focus groups there was a consensus that perhaps clergy would offer their homily time for people to reflect on their stories. When I spoke at Masses throughout the Killaloe Diocese many people remarked how it was nice to hear a different voice, and above all a female voice. On the weekends where I spoke at Masses about the future Church, the feedback was phenomenal.

People waited for me after Mass and were surprised, if not shocked by the statistics I offered. The parish priest may have been saying the same thing for months but suddenly here was a woman, a different voice speaking from the altar, telling them that the priest they had right now was likely to be the last priest in that parish. There was shock at this statement. Although people understand there is a huge fall in vocations, they somehow thought a priest would be found somewhere for them.

I would end my talk by asking, 'what would you do as a community if you no longer had a priest'. This question caused consternation.

It created a buzz and conversation for a day or two, but I suspect communities fell back into old habits not entertaining the question posed as it is too difficult to consider. Like so many clergy, parishioners are now saying 'it will see me out'. Leaders within the community struggle to counter harmful media stereotypes.
It is difficult to rise above the abuse scandals and give a vision of life that is untainted.

Our journey through history is now being rewritten. The view of tradition and doctrine has been tainted even poisoned.
It is very difficult to remain passionate and confident in the critical eyes of today. It would be a shame to have all the treasures we learned and all the beautiful traditions we lived out to be buried with us, never to be seen again. We must tell the story of our community and tell it loud and proud. After all, it is the truth that sets us free.

By using outreach, we can live out our story, invite people to events in our community. We can examine events or programmes where we can invite friends and family to share. We can look to providing speakers or programmes that inspire and awaken passion. We can look at speakers who live in the community and have faced similar struggles to those living there.

We can look at a variety of outreach programmes and provide some that are relevant and innovative. It is all about coming together.

We should lead by example and empathise with the community and their needs. Perhaps hold a seminar for the unemployed, bring in a motivational speaker on living the best life, do a workshop on household spending, have a gathering for the sick or bereaved. Meet people where they are. After all, fewer and fewer people are attending Church. There is a reason for this, it is no longer relevant in people's lives, maybe it is not engaging enough. We could make it more relevant and more engaging. Make it more welcoming. Move out from the building.

It sounds simple and it may not be perfect but if we open up to people where we work, live, and hang out together, we will build compassionate and passionate communities. The early communities started small by meeting in each other's houses and recounting their stories. They cultivated friendships. They were kind, big-hearted and welcoming.

They were charitable to others in their homes, they believed in table-ship. After all, there is no better way to get to know each other than around a table enjoying the company of others and sharing. By living good lives and sharing with others, we are opening ourselves up to be caring compassionate people. Likewise, by allowing our friends to open up, we undertake to learn more about our communities.

Together we can help each other become the best version of ourselves. We are guilty of building a whole culture based on experience but if we begin to reach out and share our story, people will respond. Here in Ireland, we have a spirit that glows with honesty, sincerity, passion, and fun.

If we could remember this and bring it forth into the community, we could experience genuine goodness.
Too many people are feeling fatigued by life and the world around them so meeting them where they are can only be a good thing. By making ourselves available to our communities, others may follow.

Lay-led Church

There is a strong desire among communities now for a lay-led Church. A new era dawns where there are fewer clergy, and this should be prepared for. There is no indication thus far that this is going to improve, therefore, the area of lay ministry could be explored.

The idea is that the laity will take on more roles and responsibilities. It is unlikely that ever before in the history of the Church has the role of the lay person been so necessary than right now. Since Vatican II, there has been a role for the laity, yet here in Ireland, there remains a basic lack of understanding of the role of the laity.

We believed for so long that the only real vocation in the Church is for the ordained. Most think the role of the laity is simply to help out around the parish. It could be to maintain and keep the Church clean or to create a nice altar and supply flowers. When Eucharist ministers were introduced, it was met with disbelief. The Church has moved on a lot since then. Many would indeed like to be much more involved. However, they are unclear on what their role might be. Lay people can bring with them different life experiences to the mission of the Church.

They can discern their calling and bring their skills and talents to the community. By "laity" the Church means 'all the faithful except those in Holy Orders and those who belong to a religious state'.

The laity has its part to play in the mission of the Church and the World. It is true the laity are not priests but that does not mean they do not care what happens to our Church or community. They are participants in fulfilling the mission of the Church.

It is a major error to think that only those called to religious or clerical life have a vocation.

The vocation as laypeople stems from Baptism and is strengthened through our Confirmation. Each has been called to their vocation and mission. Priests and laity work together as members of the Church. A future can be provided for the Church if all work together in collaboration. The church is no longer the focal point of the community, but it still has its place.

Even though the role of the laity is equal, the role of the ordained is distinct. I read once that 'in the Church there is a diversity of ministry but a oneness of mission'. This is a wonderful example of how it should be. Everyone has unique roles. The priest has his at the altar and the laity have theirs out in the world of community. There is no need to wait around for 'Father's' permission or 'to ask Father'. Community leaders can be at the frontline, reimaging their future in this modern world and making sure the community becomes a centre of formation and empowerment for all. We should not be waiting for bishops and priests to provide formation as we are responsible for our education, our formation, our communities. It is down to us to know and live our own lives. People are more interested than ever in living their best lives, constantly searching.

Pastoral workers can be the link between the laity and the clergy. Ultimately, the church should be guided to a certain point by the congregation. Having ministry teams shaped around the needs of the community and its members would be a great way forward. The ministry could be a music ministry, a children's ministry, a liturgical ministry, youth ministry, ministry of the word, Eucharistic ministry, funeral ministry, prayers ministry, maintenance ministry, altar ministry, caretaking ministry and much more. Each ministry is responsible for its own designated activity within the community providing the training and resources needed. The word ministry can be very scary to lay people as it has always been associated with clergy and very special holy people. However, all are special.

It would be wonderful if members of the community could be given the space and resources to offer their concepts to the community. No one person has all the gifts but those who have unique gifts should be given the space and freedom to explore how they can contribute.
Perhaps we should entertain the notion of conducting get-togethers or workshops to help people identify the gifts they have. The main challenge at present is for people to find time to get involved. Even with all the support and resources in place, it is difficult to find the people to get involved. But we cannot give up. We need to remain hopeful. Hopeful of building resilient, inclusive communities into the future.

For those who attend Church, their number one expectation is to have a lovely spiritual experience. People want to experience belonging and a strong connectedness. This means being open to change.

Many clergies are ready for change, but the laity is struggling. They are accustomed to turning up with everything provided. This is no longer possible as our clergy cannot be all things to all people all the time.

Communities can be role models. People need role models who live life in the way they do. They need someone who shares their pain and shares their dreams.

This is a way we can support each other, care for each other, give each other strength. Looking to others who have similar stories to ourselves is not only interesting but also inspiring and motivating. Many feel they are not qualified to share their story. We do not all need degrees or PhDs to be a vital part of our community. Putting our life experience to good use is much more beneficial than any piece of paper you have gained.

Reaching out is important for ourselves and our community. Showing love and compassion is a significant qualification when getting involved in the community. Sometimes we need to trust people, let go, give people the opportunity to share pastoral care. People want positive experiences for their families and their communities.

Pastoral care is a huge part of this, as is feeling connected to each other. Friendships do not automatically grow but by sharing and growing together we will develop a strong connectedness and deep friendships. If the community can create opportunities and generate openings for people to get together, they will help build a robust community.

Gathering the laity for ministry can ease some of the burdens on the clergy. There is so much a lay person can do. Many of our parishes here in Ireland are beginning the journey of building lay ministry.

When the Church is centred around one person it puts a lot of pressure on that individual but when it is shared out among many it is much healthier. We have many communities now in Ireland that no longer have a resident priest. These Churches are strongly dependent on the local community.

Many found themselves without a priest before they were prepared. These communities are inspiring.

They were upset because their community was left without a resident priest, but it strengthened their resolve in their own ability to get things done. It also allowed them to mould their community going forward. Everyone had a role to play. As a child in Broadford, we attended every service in the Church. Attendance at Church was how its success was measured.

It is not about the number of people there, but by the experience they have. The experience needs to be awe-inspiring, to encourage people to return. As I visited all parishes in Clare, I was greatly encouraged by the number of initiatives already in existence. So much work, time, and energy have gone into their way forward. I was lucky to meet dedicated people at workshops and gatherings I organized throughout the diocese. I felt lucky so many fully participated in these nights. By working together, we can face the challenges of the future. We can contribute to shaping our communities in a new way.

Listen to all the voices

When we discuss women and their role in the Church, we are inclined to concentrate almost wholly on the ordination of women. I feel, however, the debate is much, much, deeper than that. We as women have a vocation. We all need to grow in our understanding that we have a voice. Women are full members of the community and the Church. A lot of headway has been made in recent years, but we still have a long way to go. There is a need for greater cooperation.

Women are already doing a lot in their communities, but they do it in silence. They are there continuously.

When we look at our history, women were invisible, they did not count. There were many great women in our society, but they were written out of history. We live in what was a patriarchal society and although things have moved on dramatically, we still live in what Ursula Barry calls a 'gender skewed society'. In Ireland, we have a constant struggle with equality.

Women and men have so strongly internalized the patriarchal stereotype that it is deeply ingrained in our psyche.

We are still journeying towards a society where women and men are equal and where there is widespread respect for diversity. We can only continue to move forward and look to the future of our daughters. My daughters are already living in a better world than I did.

Many women continue to sustain the Church, but nobody knows about it. They serve silently and diligently, and this must be valued.

There are calls by many for the ordination of women but not every woman wants to be a priest or be ordained but all like to be appreciated. Many women are working away in the background, but they feel unheard and unappreciated. The discussion on women in the Church has been fairly limited so far but one thing is for certain, we are only beginning to scratch the surface. Pope Francis has made great efforts to bring the plight of the poor and the marginalized to the attention of the church. Although he has spoken about the role of women, he has not made any great strides in this direction.

There are more and more women taking part in theological and religious courses.

Changing the concepts and the structures of the Church can only be a good thing. Having a deeper appreciation of who we are will enable all of us to begin to change the age-old image of male domination. Women's creativity and imagination as well as their warmth can open new ways of being church and new ways of being community. Men and women together can inspire communities for the benefit of all. Women can be very resilient in many areas, especially in conflict. They are very good at working together in the face of adversity. By nature, they are caretakers.

Having been involved with the Church all my life I sometimes feel very let down.

From what I've read, the early church was very much pro-woman, they were appreciated and listened to. Listening to the gospels we can see they are not anti-woman. Yet the Magisterium, the teaching authority of the Church, is composed of men, why and when did this happen.

There should be more women's voices in the Church and this is just not my consensus but that of many. Women have the authority to represent Christ in every area of their life if they wish. Focusing on women priests can take away from all the good work they are already doing within the Church. There are some women's voices in the Church, but they are difficult to find.

The pope says that women do 'many things better than men' but this praise for women gives little comfort to those dedicated who want a more influential role.

The church has continually reacted to criticism of the ban on women by saying that Jesus only chose men as his apostles. That was then and this is now, a very different time.

This question of women's inequality in the Church continues to be a hot topic. Patriarchy and hierarchy have hurt in the past. The damaging results of the oppressive structures have been felt. Women have been waiting for their voices to be heard for centuries.

I fear the time will come when we get fed up with waiting and those voices will be lost forever. The conversation on expanding women's leadership in the church needs to intensify. Most would agree that 80% of work done in the Church is done by women. If women are not given the opportunities to grow within the Church they will be lost forever.

Opportunities are opening up in the secular world to women: it is slow, but it is happening, so why not in the Church? I am not talking about ordination here but there are many opportunities where women could be appointed to leadership roles. They could share their personal stories as it is women who dominate the caring world. It is women who could help build a more human, caring community.

Many courageous women have inspiring life stories on how they overcame adversity. These stories could be an immense inspiration to others.

If we could have women deacons like the early Church maybe their stories could be heard. As the early Church grew, the apostles were not able to attend to all its ministries. This was when the diaconate was created. We should note, therefore, that the diaconate was a creation of the Church. The first deacons were called by the apostles, not by Jesus. Perhaps what the Church created the Church can amend. For many centuries, the Church ordained women to the diaconate. Consequently, you would think what the Church did in the past, it could do again.

The diaconate is a separate ministry and there is no reason in my mind why women cannot be deacons.

Women deacons in the early Church were directed at women and children as no man could anoint a woman. These were different times but there is no reason why we cannot learn from the past to inform the future. As the early Church became more formalized male and female deacons were ordained by the bishop. As women of the early Church served clerical roles, why can they not do so now? In 1 Timothy 3:11 Paul writes of the conditions needed to be a woman deacon they 'must be respectable, no gossips but sober and quite reliable'.

In Romans 16:1-2 we are told about Phoebe who is 'a deacon of the Church in Cenchreae'. Some would argue that these women were not sacramentally ordained, but this begs the question, would the early Church bishop allow sacred acts to be performed by a person who was not ordained? I think not, as these Bishops were very devout and followed the rules religiously.

Why then, has this form of thought been lost to our Church. Some say that women who are debating the reinstatement of women deacons are power-hungry.

What then does that say about priests? We are all called to serve not to wield power. The Irish Bishops Conference requested permission from Rome to ordain permanent deacons. Many dioceses now have permanent deacons in training or already working. These, however, are all men. By all means, have male deacons but open it up to women who would also like to enrich the Church with their ministry. Some will argue that appointing more priests is the only answer, but surely with our growth and progression since the early Church, we can be more creative than that. The Church needs the ministry of all.

While working with the Diocese of Killaloe it was announced that the diocese was planning to introduce the Permanent Diaconate. People were invited to come forward but again it was only open to men. This came as a surprise to those who had worked for the years previous on a listening process. This listening process was very extensive and at no point were Permanent Diaconate mentioned. This process resulted in the drawing up of the Diocesan Pastoral Plan, Builders of Hope: 2013-2020. This plan is based on the participation of all those involved in the Church in the Killaloe Diocese.

On hearing that their Diocese was now looking for Permanent Diaconates some women in the Diocese acted immediately in expressing their frustration with the decision. They called a public meeting which was very well attended with a cross-section of people from across the Diocese.

The evening was well organised, and everyone was given the chance to speak regardless of their views. The women on the night spoke about how the work proposed to be done by deacons was already being done by women.
They felt the Permanent Diaconate was simply another layer of clericalism. The then Bishop took note of what was happening, and the proposal was put on hold.

This night demonstrated the enormous power women have when they come together. Both the men and the women who spoke on that night did so in an articulate, coherent manner. There is a need for Diaconate, and it would be great if it were available to anyone who wanted it, whether male or female.

I think it can safely be said that the introduction of the Permanent Diaconate in the

Killaloe Diocese is off the agenda for now. In a way this is sad. Many would like to play a greater part in their church, and it should be open to them whether they are men or women.

It should be all about supporting each other. We should all be charged with the Church's charity not just the few. We do not have to be male or female to visit the sick and imprisoned, to provide food and clothing for those in need, or to oversee our local Church. The Irish bishops' note that one of the reasons to re-establish the permanent diaconate in Ireland is to make sacred ministers available where there is a shortage of clergy.

When most people think about the Catholic Church, they focus on the Roman or Latin Church. The Catholic Church formally acknowledges the authority of the Orthodox Churches, and they approve the ordination of women deacons. The question is, can this be open to women as well as men? On the other hand, should we exclude men because women are excluded? The debate needs to happen. Unfortunately, it seems to be a case of kicking the can down the road or the 'it will see me out' attitude.

I once heard Dr Phyllis Zagano, a leading expert on women deacons and the Catholic Church speak, she said 'I have been constantly told by people working in the Vatican that they can't say no to women deacons, they just don't want to say yes'. It has been reported that Pope Francis told bishops' conferences around the world if they wanted something, they just had to ask. Deacons could bring the Church in Ireland new life, at least it is worth talking about.

There is also an ongoing debate surrounding the 'roles' or 'callings' of men and women in the Church.

All by virtue of baptism, are called to serve nonetheless some are expected to serve in silence. I was at a meeting once where a woman who was extremely passionate about her calling said that 'it was a shame she was missing an appendage that would give her a greater voice in her beloved Church'. There was a sharp intake of breath from those in attendance, but it demonstrated her and others exasperation at not being heard.

Across the board, women's voices are still very under-represented.

Giving women key positions in all areas of society is good for everybody.

They are good at opening dialogue and finding a compromise where men sometimes become deadlocked. Allowing everyone to express their journey, can only benefit the whole community. It would be good to remember that the ordained members of our community are not the only ones on a faith journey.

They may bring different gifts and talents, but they are not on a better or more important journey than anyone else. People have grown up with their own history of the Church, their own understanding of tradition which shapes and guides them. We have a division of clergy and laity.

In the past, it was considered that the laity was less informed, less qualified members of the Church. This can no longer be considered the case, as so many are educated in theology. Indeed, many are more educated in theology than some priests.

Perhaps all look at themselves as disciples, lay disciples, ordained disciples, male disciples, female disciples. This would put all on an even keel. This would promote equality. It would make communities much more inclusive. The Greek word 'Ekklesia' was the word used to denote the first

104

followers of the Church. It signified the assembled community of equal disciples. This was how the Church was seen for the first few decades.

The institutionalization of the Church, however, rendered women invisible. Paul said at one point 'let the women be silent': all these centuries later it looks like we have Paul to blame for our lack of voice. At this point I feel the need to say, as a woman who worked within the Church both voluntary and paid, I felt my voice was heard by those around me. I worked with over one hundred priests and by and large, most of them promoted the elevation of women's voices.

Despite this, I feel the institutional Church does not feel the contribution of women is required for the development of the Church. This is a mistake. The Church is being kept alive by women at parochial level. If there is no local Church, there will be no need for a hierarchy, as there will be no chain to command. Women are more than half the population so why then is there no female representation in history? It seems the Church does not know what to do with women.

When asked about the ordination of women most Church officials just say 'the door is closed on that issue'. They do not know what else to say.

The Catholic Church tends to support women's equal access to education, employment, and political participation. Despite this, it does not promote equal rights within its own confines. I first noticed inequality when my brother was accepted to be an altar server, but girls were not allowed. Girls were confined to being in the choir or to reading. They were relegated to a supporting role. As I got older, I got very frustrated with what appeared to me as the Church's lack of compassion.

It fails more than half its parishioners. I thought about leaving but someone needs to ask the questions.

I was questioning to ensure a new Church, one that recognizes the full equality of all its members. It's too late for my daughters, intelligent, kind, young women who have chosen not to stay where they are seen as subordinate.

Pope Francis is a breath of fresh air for the church. I like him, but it was he who declared the door to ordaining women priests was 'closed.'

The representation of women at hierarchical gatherings is still low.

In 2015 at the Synod on the Family, there were thirty women out of approximately three hundred and sixty attendees, and they could not vote. Change is needed.

An end to oppressive, unfair practices that consign women to second class status is needed.

I have a vision where my Church honours women's rights to make decisions that affect my life. A Church that welcomes everyone. I fear this is too late even for me as I am optimistic, but I am tired of the same excuses. My energy is best used elsewhere.

Chapter Three

Purpose: Mission and Spirituality

"Welcome, O life! I go to encounter for the
millionth time the reality of experience and to
forge in the smithy of my soul the uncreated
conscience of my race."
James Joyce

Finding Purpose

Finding our purpose in life entails discovering what makes us tick. It gives us a reason to get up in the morning. Purpose is unique for all of us. We just need to find the motivating aims of our lives. Sounds simple but it can be difficult for many. Our path may be different from others. Our purpose may shift and change throughout our lives. It may depend on our evolving priorities as well as the variations of our life experiences.

One of the greatest questions in life is how we find our purpose. Maybe the best way is through self-examination or soul searching. Plunging deeply into the spirit of who we are will help us in putting together all the pieces. Finding our life's purpose is a journey of sorts. It is part of our heart's desire to always want to improve. We want more enthusiasm, more drive, more determination, and more fullness. We all want to live better and more fruitful lives. How fantastic would it be to wake up every morning, jump out of bed, feeling excited about the day ahead? This is a feeling we all want. Most of us want to make our mark on the world. We want to make a difference.

Finding our purpose could be the guiding force of this. Perhaps we need to decide what difference do we want to make? Looking inwardly can be a difficult task and may bring up things from our past we would rather forget but being at peace with our past may help us find our purpose. Knowing ourselves inside and out and being self-aware is important. Initially, we may be resistant but in persisting we will find the courage to face our inner demons.

Shining a spotlight on those demons will help us move forward. There may be times when you feel you will never find your purpose.

Your inner voice may be telling you 'You don't deserve it'. This is natural. Pay attention to your thoughts, be aware, acknowledge them and finally, they will lose their control over you. As soon as you become familiar with your inner demons it will become easier to slay them. I found the best way to slay them is to act despite them. Knowing yourself inside and out is power building. In baring your soul to yourself you become a better person and it will help you on your road to self-discovery and your purpose in life.

When we are afraid of moving forward or something is holding us back, it is good to take a deep breath, acknowledge the feeling and do it anyway. This way you are blazing a trail for your future. To find our purpose we should find what sets our soul on fire. Creating space in our lives where we can, mull over these questions would be beneficial. Try not to be judgmental of ourselves. There are enough people out there who will do that for us but ignore them. When we find our true selves, all those around us will benefit.

Once we figure out our greatest motivations, we will learn to guide our life in a new direction. We all had passions when we were younger, but most of us had to give them up for practical reasons, but maybe we can reimagine our passion. Connect once more to our inner child, take a stroll down memory lane, and work out what brought us joy. For me it was writing, it was acting, and it was being with people. As a child I wrote little stories for family, I put on shows, I had an amazing imagination. Returning to these passions brings me great joy.

I know being a mother and being of service to people as well as writing is my life's purpose. I feel it in my bones that making people happy is what I really want to do. This may not be your course but finding the path that is unique to you will bring you happiness and purpose.

Creating goals and finding purpose may connect us with our community. Connecting to the people in our community can be very meaningful and satisfying. We all seek meaning. Many seek it through spirituality or religious beliefs. Many through art, dance music, creativity. Only we know what will drive us. Many are uncertain about pursuing their purpose because they feel it sounds conceited or self-serving. But this is not the case. It is good to recognize our gifts and talents and contribute them to the community. This allows our purpose in life to evolve. It is important to continue evolving. Continue growing. Continue going forward.

By living our purpose, we feel alive. We feel fully connected. We feel we belong. Finding purpose offers many benefits especially psychologically. Purpose motivates us daily. Having a sense of meaning is crucial to our survival. Dr Viktor Frankl who wrote Man's Search for Meaning, said that even in the most miserable of situations, referring to the 'Holocaust', a person could live a meaningful life.

Finding Purpose – can benefit our community

In this modern world, with our busy lives, it can be very difficult to find time to get involved in the community. However, the rewards of connecting with others and getting involved with the community can be immense. It can help you fulfil your purpose in life.

Helping others will help your community and will provide you with a valued sense of purpose.

Giving to your community, even in simple ways, will help, and in the process improve your happiness. Studies have shown that the more people volunteered, the happier they were. Volunteering in the community connects us with others and is good for our minds bringing fun and fulfilment. One of the better-known benefits of volunteering is the effect on the community. Connecting to the community makes it a better place for everyone. Helping in the smallest way can make a real difference.

It will help make new friends, increase networks, further social skills and fulfil our purpose in life. It is well known that one of the best ways to make new friends and to give a boost to existing friendships is to carry out a shared activity. Getting involved in the community is a great way to meet people. It strengthens our community ties and increases the resources of the community. Sharing gifts and talents with the community can only benefit all involved.

Volunteering allows developing as a person and helps with finding fulfilment. The social aspect of working with others can have an overwhelming effect. Meaningful connections reduce stress and improve mood. This can only be advantageous to all. Researchers found that in being helpful to others we can find meaning. Human beings are hard-wired to give. In giving we feel more at peace with ourselves.

In doing good for others and the community we increase self-confidence and build self-esteem. The better you feel about yourself, the more likely you are to reach your future goals and realise your life purpose. Becoming involved in the community provides a sense of purpose. A sense of meaning.

It allows practising many important skills such as teamwork, communication, problem-solving, as well as project planning and organization.

In turn, the community benefits from renewed creativity, motivation, and vision. By matching your gifts, talents, goals, and interests to your community, you are most likely to have fun and be fulfilled.

The community is enhanced when volunteers participate in clean-ups, gardening, and planting. It also benefits from volunteers who provide day care and eldercare. Schools are developed and strengthened when volunteers give their time and resources. Providing after school programs can be of huge benefit to the area. It helps build the self-esteem and personal growth of youth and it encourages them to become solid members of the community volunteering themselves.

Interaction between people from a variety of backgrounds working toward a common goal helps build solidarity. It promotes solidarity and harmony for all. When a community is pulling together everyone tends to thrive and the community finds purpose.

When like-minded people share their talents, gifts, values, and goals they can create a new future. The hearts and souls of the many can collectively make a difference. They can ultimately change the world. As the saying goes, 'It takes a village to raise a child'. Well, it takes a community of like-minded people to generate energy and sustain itself into the future. Communities face many challenges but the potential to grow is immense if they find purpose. Growing and sustaining into the future is about reaching past all the barriers. In identifying our purpose in life, we will be able to meet and greet the challenges posed to our communities.

Our mission

After a time of continuous fall-off in most Western countries, we need to ask whether our tight-knit communities will be able to exist into the future. There is one thing for certain we need to step up to our responsibility. If we do not, we will lose an important part of our heritage and our tradition. What will we hand on to those coming after us?

We are in a time of materialism where 'things' and 'appearances' have become increasingly important. We are building a society on 'appearances'. This may look good but what if we scratch the surface? Will we find substance? It is also a time of seeking. A time of inquiry. A time of looking for fulfilment. Can we help our communities find this fulfilment? And, if so, how? This is an issue that needs to be explored.

If the Church is to re-establish itself, it will have to be a new type of church and one that is more involved in outreach. More community-minded. During recent visits with Pastoral Councils, it became obvious that some people want to return to the past. Many voices asked, 'how do we get the youth back into the Church' and they were very upset when I said, 'that is unlikely to happen.' In my opinion, we are not going to get the youth back in the Church. We should be bringing the Church to them.

The past is past and if we are honest, it wasn't always that great anyway. We need to find a new way forward. The question is how do we do that? There are many difficulties to this. As already stated, some people are stuck in the past and are resistant to change.

Others are no longer churchly by birth and the institution itself has trouble adjusting to its new situation. Many are like the apostles when Jesus was taken to be crucified, they went into hiding. Are we hiding from the truth? We are hiding because we do not know how to react.

The mission handed on to us humans is to take care of and transform the world in which we live. This is a continuous challenge. It is so easy for us to think that our time is more problematic and more challenging than other times in history. Nonetheless, all periods of history have had outstanding challenges. Our time is no different. We all think that our time is unique and that our situation is exceptional, but it is not. We must deal with the same questions and challenges in every age. How we face those challenges is what is different. It is up to us to leave the world a better place because we were there. Make our mark regardless of how small.

To move forward we should draw on the wisdom of the past, but this does not mean going back to the familiar. We should embrace change and move forward. All of us have a desire, a yearning for happiness and peace of mind. A spiritual existence. In this materialistic world, inner peace can be difficult to find. Actions in the community may give the opportunity to find that fulfilment.

In putting into words, the significance of community in the modern world, we ought to be bold, brilliant, creative, and above all, inspiring. People need to be inspired to get involved. This all sounds very simple. But it is far from simple. The very best of people involved in the community find it difficult to work out where this inspiration might come from. They want practical answers. As do those involved in Church.

It was my experience that those involved in Church at every level were tired of conversation and they wanted practical ways of embracing change. However, the conversation can be ongoing but there is no reason why we cannot walk and talk at the same time.

In this section of the book, through research and talking with people, I intend to consider practical steps that can be explored in our communities. We first need to look at our mission. All of us together share in the mission of our community. When we think of mission we think of our religious and clergy who went to serve overseas.

Many will also associate mission with priests, usually Redemptorists who arrived in our parish for a week to give talks and sermons to the local community. I remember them coming to Broadford. They were very effective. It was usually a unique week in the local calendar. A time of unity for all. The church was filled every night to listen to the speakers.

Many communities across the diocese have endeavoured to hold a mission in recent times. They were well-attended. I was surprised by this as I honestly thought mission would be seen as an outdated model of coming together. However, the speakers were relevant, and people related to them. Sometimes we do not need to reinvent the wheel, we just need to be open to the experience. We all have different vocations, and it is down to us to live them out. My vocation has been as a daughter, a sister, a mother, a teacher, and a pastoral worker. I gave each vocation my all. It was my vocation as a mother that I am most proud of.

Parish Councils used to think they were all about maintenance. Looking after the finances and structures, keeping the grass cut and the roofs fixed but with the change from Parish Councils to Pastoral Councils there is a need to change from maintenance to mission. This is a difficult transition for many. Of course, maintenance is important but striking a balance is equally important.

Mission can be understood in many ways. While facilitating a workshop on 'maintenance v mission' in the Diocese of Killaloe, Pastoral Councils had various ways of looking at it. The majority saw it as reaching out to the community. Reaching out to the marginalised, to elderly, to youth, to single parents. One Pastoral Council identified a need to provide something for bereaved families and they initiated the training and setting up of a bereavement group.

Another Pastoral Council concentrated on volunteers and provided an evening of affirmation and appreciation for them. Another community recognised their need as youth, and they undertook an extensive youth programme. Throughout these workshops, Pastoral Councils admitted to being stuck in maintenance but they resolved to take time as a leadership group to give considerable time to their discernment of mission and what it means to them and their community. This is a journey of discovery for Parish Pastoral Councils. As a community leadership group, it is good to be concerned with ongoing formation. All must move forward together striving to be vibrant, animated communities.

Spirituality is at the heart of mission. Mission is not a matter of doing things for people. It is about connecting with and being with people. It is good to be open to others as well as being open to change. Present our life through our words and our actions. In living a good life, we can share that with our communities.

We learn from each other, and we may not always get it right, but it's about trying. It's about opening our hearts to our surroundings. In embracing our community, we will be nourished. In having shared respectfulness and dignity for each other we move from maintenance (doing things for others) to mission (doing things with others). We can empower each other. We can all enjoy a feeling of belonging. I often speak with confirmation children, and we discuss believing and belonging. It is a session I love doing with them and it is a session they really enjoy. Children are so open and love their community.

The Diocese of Killaloe has used clustering as a way forward. Where groups of parishes are clustered together to share resources. This is a new way of seeing community. Working together can be a useful tool as it includes many other talented and gifted people. Cluster has now become pastoral areas and it reminds us that community is bigger than just our parish.

Many are finding it difficult to get their heads around cluster as they are very committed to the local community and local Church. Some have energy for local, some for cluster and others for national. Each one is important in different ways. Being in a cluster reminds us of the importance of carrying out our mission together. Clustering allows us to link with other communities thus enabling all to build on the wider resources. It is beneficial for neighbouring parishes to come together to see what they can do together throughout the year.

While facilitating workshops in the Diocese of Killaloe, parishes met in clusters. This was a very useful exercise as those attending felt that sharing in the same event made them feel more empowered.

As the gatherings were accompanied by a cup of tea and a chat, it allowed those present to mingle, get to know each other and learn from the challenges and triumphs of the other parishes. These gatherings brought with them a great sense of togetherness and inspiration.

Although parishes border each other, they can be very different and this can be a learning for others. Many future possibilities were discussed. Some parishes chose to share baptism teams and liturgy groups. Some felt they needed further training and decided to come together to organise that. Others decided they would hold a cross-cluster event. There are fifty-eight parishes divided into twelve clusters in the Diocese of Killaloe. Each cluster is unique in its own way. It may have a different way of working depending on the number of parishes involved and the geographical area. While working here I found it difficult to tell if cluster was working, but there are very few alternative options.

Local Church is still of immense importance with cluster at its infancy. All involved at cluster level should be clear about their future goals and agree on how they are realised.

Communities are experiencing times of struggle and challenge. The despair and confusion caused were not of our making, yet we are the ones left to mend bridges and move forward. If we can do this by remaining true to our tradition and ritual, we will achieve something wonderful. I feel we can pull this off in our lifetime if we want to. I firmly believe we can keep the rituals and traditions of our ancestors alive. It may not be in the way we have developed them over the decades but in a new, exciting, and creative way.

So many now look to spirituality and have become once more interested in pilgrimage, Mass Rocks and ancient monuments. There are so many places here in Ireland where we can feel connected. Where we can sense those who went before us. Where we can find that inner peace that eludes so many of us. In most of our communities, we can find sacred, special, and meaningful places. Exploring the possibilities and reviving some ancient traditions could be the answer to nurturing our own communities. A willingness to work collectively and creatively would ensure strong communities into the future.

Our Moral Compass

I often feel that we are morally drifting within our communities. Do we really understand or care what is going on in the world around us? Listening to the news and learning what is going on in our society can be very disheartening. We are fundamentally moral, but we sometimes lack a compass or a foundational guide. Whether or not we are involved in organized religion we can look to our community to find such a moral grounding. We all have a conscience, having the inner sense of what is right and wrong comes to most of us. It is cultivated in our homes and nourished in our communities. Community, therefore, is very important to us. We grow up in our communities learning social skills and learning right from wrong.

Our parents are our first teachers, and our communities are our next. We were given the freedom to create and live our own lives and make our own moral decisions. Many of us do not seem to know where we belong.

We do not seem to know if we are doing the right thing with our lives. I, for example, have changed the direction of my life many times and each time I used my conscience as a compass. Sometimes I got it right and sometimes I got it wrong but each time, I gained an education. Each time I broadened my horizons. Each time I got experience. For me, the worst possible thing in life would be to remain stuck.

Some feel our youth have no moral compass. That they are following a poorly-defined, weak, and loose moral individualism. I for one think our youth are fantastic. It is my experience through working with young people and raising young adults that although they may not attend Church, they are morally robust. They grow up in communities that are immersed in moral traditions and some of this must seep through.

We as communities need to nurture this youth and find ways of meeting them where they are at. Yes, some make up their own rules but the vast majority examine their conscience and live by their moral guidelines. I find young people happy to engage in discussions about real moral dilemmas. By demonstrating moral values in our communities, we can help guide the creation of better and more just societies. We can be a positive example to our young people.

I believe from my engagement with local communities that they are willing to engage in an active search to find ways to help. Our youth experience their development and strength through their community. Communities can be successful in protecting youth from at-risk behaviour if they provide an all-round healthy and nurturing environment. Giving them somewhere they can be together in harmony, a wholesome community benefits and protects all.

Supportive and caring families are foremost in making a difference in the lives of youth. Nonetheless, proactive communities that provide space for youth can be equally effective. Providing different spaces and different activities will further the variety of gifts, skills, and talents of all who take part. Separate community strengths may not on their own have a remarkable impact, but they become formidable when drawn together. Bring youth into our decision making. Make them increasingly visible and active as it will contribute to the development of our community and the psychological development of everyone involved.

Inspiring our youth to become involved in the community adds to their moral reasoning and their overall value system. This can only be a good thing in the short term as well as the long term.

Our Spirituality

'Spirituality' signifies the virtues that inspire and motivate us to do what is right and good. Compassion and justice are spiritual talents we use for the benefit of community. Being compassionate makes us more effective. Being active entails having talent and skills and using them. Spirituality could be brought to the community in an enthusiastic, warm and supportive way. The focus is not so much on the skill but more on the 'spirit.' The spirit brought from within. The spirit to encourage others. The spirit to inspire others to participate. The spirit to advocate and support a good cause. This spirit seems elusive but that does not mean we should not try to understand it.

Spiritual people have a presence, and it can bring a strong influence to the community.

Being a spiritual person, having spiritual qualities empowers us to do what is right and good both for ourselves and for our community. Bringing compassion and kindness to the community is for the good of all.

Having a compassionate and forgiving nature is something that is extensively valued by others. They can be found in every community and are valued in every tradition. A person does not have to be religious to have these qualities. Spiritual people inspire us to do what is good. Bringing our spirit to those around us can only have positive results. It helps build a better world. Respecting others and their spirituality can support us in fostering our own spirituality. We can become the change agent for the betterment of our communities.

It seems reasonable that certain types of spiritual gifts and talents can enable the community more than others. If a person finds it difficult to empathise with others, they will not understand their suffering and will be unable to act to support them. In building strong communities, we need kind, compassionate people to take the lead. Those active in the community are generally aware of the needs of others. Finding common bonds within the community is important.

Making contact with others, even by saying 'hello' or a 'nod of the head' shows appreciation of that other person. Small encounters not only give us a sense of belonging but help others feel they belong also. A sense of belonging is essential to mental health. Every day when I walk the dog I nod and smile at everyone I meet, not only am I increasing my physical health, but I feel great after my walk. I feel I belong in the community. I feel respected. We should all get out in our communities and share our spirit.

Having something positive to say to others in our community shows kindness and caring. All the little actions add up and have a collective effect on the community. Sharing kindness with others makes for a caring, happy, healthy community.

We hear about the importance of having a spiritual practice, but what does that mean? Why is it important, and how do we weave a spiritual practise into our daily life? For me, spirituality involves examining how we relate to the world around us as well as how we commune with our sense of self. Spirituality and religion do not have to be one and the same thing. For me, there is no 'right' way to be spiritual. It is about what speaks to you, what enables you to find meaning and purpose in life, and is a pathway to connect with the world around you and beyond.

I would suggest that spirituality is about how we get out of our heads and into our souls. It can originate anywhere. It is a sense of energy that connects all living things. Community, connection, and a sense of purpose are the foundations upon which we build our lives. It is important to discover a sense of belonging, rather than feel disconnected and alone.

Through spirituality, we can let go of ourselves and find a sense of connectivity and belonging. It helps us feel good about ourselves. It helps us live in the moment and become mindful of our inner-self and our impact on those around us. Spirituality has a positive impact on nearly every aspect of life. Studies show that people who have a spiritual practice, experience physical health benefits as well mental ones.

As we become mindful of self-care and the importance of nurturing loving-kindness towards ourselves and others, we begin to feel healthier, exercise more, and get more sleep, all beneficial to our physical wellbeing. I am not a lover of the phrase 'me time' as that sounds selfish. Self-care is essential to our health, but it is not necessarily about being alone. It may mean a coffee with a friend or spending time with loved ones. Nonetheless, it is good to spend time with yourself if possible.

Beginning a spiritual practice may not be easy but neither is it difficult. It is important to remember that you find a practice that works for you. Everyone is unique and as such every spiritual practice is unique. For me I find taking time to sit and be, lets me tune in to my spiritual self. A daily meditation practice can enable you to become more self-aware. There are many meditation methods, but the most important aspect is to carve a peaceful time out of each day, find a comfortable space and focus on yourself and your breathing.

Several years ago, I went in search of a space that gave me a sense of peace, I felt sitting in a church could bring the silence and freedom I needed. However, I did not find that in my own parish church, but I found it very close by. I found it in St Flannan's Cathedral Killaloe, the Church of Ireland. I felt at one with myself and all those who had gone before me. It took me a long time to find the inner peace I craved but within these walls I let the thoughts and emotions come and go.

Finally, I managed to notice these feelings without judgement. The idea is to develop the ability to simply 'be' and stay fully present in your mind and body. I was able to do this in St Flannan's. I believe it is because of its historical significance. Early in the twelfth century, Donal Mor O'Brien, founder of St Mary's Cathedral in Limerick, built a church in Killaloe. This was replaced by the present Cathedral in approximately 1200 and is now dedicated to St Flannan, an eighth-century ancestor of Donal Mór. It dates from the transition between the Romanesque and Gothic periods, but its style is mainly Gothic with traces of earlier styles.

Up to the nineteenth century, the South Transept was used as the Bishop's Court. Here penalties for various offences were dealt out. A sinner had to do 'a public penance' in the Cathedral, bare-legged and bareheaded in a white sheet and make an open confession of his crime in a prescribed form of words.

This is a building that feels and listens. It has for hundreds of years, and it continues to do so. I for one am very glad the walls do not talk.

Guided meditations are useful if you are a beginner, but you will soon get the hang of it. Another simple practice I find very helpful is a daily gratitude list or journal to remind yourself of all the good things in your life. Even on tough days, there are things to be grateful for, and a daily gratitude reminder boosts your sense of self and helps foster a sense of loving-kindness towards yourself and others.

Yoga is another tool to bring you into the moment, focus on breath, become mindful of the body, and connect with your concept of spirituality. I am a complete beginner at yoga but already I am finding it beneficial. Many people find spirituality in beauty, such as communing with nature by taking a walk, appreciating a beautiful piece of art, or listening to music. Beauty can act as a doorway into spirituality and your sense of self. The concept is to be fully present for all these experiences, practice being still, and appreciate things that are bigger than you.

Connecting with your community will also help you thrive spiritually.

Having a solid foundation of interest in your surroundings is highly beneficial. I live my life now loving my surroundings and I hope my contribution to my community is as beneficial to others as it is to me.

St Flannan's Cathedral Killaloe, Co. Clare
(Photo Kerry Blake)

Vocations – not only for priests

When we talk about vocations, we immediately think priesthood, but we all have vocations. We have a vocation to live our best lives. To live lives that are true to ourselves. We are all unique with our own talents and skills. My vocation is, as a daughter, a mother, a sister, a friend. It is also to use my life experience to help others. Determining vocations is for everyone.

Our job or profession is not our vocation but who we are and being true to who we are is our vocation. There is no better way of living life than to live it to the fullest all the while being of service to others and our community.

If you do not know who you really are maybe it's time to begin that conversation with yourself. Take time in silence, open your heart, reflect, and listen. Trust, have faith in yourself and wait. Our answer comes from those around us, our deeds and something that touches our heart. Be patient. It may take many changes of direction before finally finding where we are most happy. Where we are most at ease.

Where we feel most peaceful. The literal meaning of the word vocation is a 'call.' Your vocation is not the same as your career, nonetheless, there may be an overlap. We all need a career to support ourselves. We can choose different careers and change them as and when we wish. However, when it comes to our vocation it is about being true to ourselves.

Our vocation is often rooted in our tradition. It is a call to love and serve our families and communities.

Desiring to be true to yourself brings an understanding that there is a reason for existence. We all long for meaning in our lives. We all need purpose.

Be open to loving. We all want to find happiness. Loving our neighbour is great but more importantly, we need to love ourselves. By making a personal commitment to put our life at the service of others, we will become true to ourselves. We are all called to model our lives on goodness, opening our hearts and finding true inner peace. Each vocation, religious or not, is a commitment to love. With that love, we can help build better communities. Pope John Paul II wrote, 'Love makes us seek what is good; love makes us better persons. It is love that prompts men and women to marry and form a family, to have children. It is love that prompts others to embrace the consecrated life or become priests'.

There is no better feeling than living our best life. We should not be happy following the path of least resistance. We should challenge ourselves to explore our full potential. Find guidance if need be, but remain active in living our true lives. It is not always easy to be true to ourselves and it can be difficult to live life the way we want. Very often it is easier to follow the crowd but recognising we are unique with unique talents will bring inner peace and harmony.

Ogham Stone
St Flannan's
Killaloe
Co. Clare

Chapter Four

Community:Tradition and Values

'I believe we are put here to improve civilisation'.
Seamus Heaney

The Core of Community Life

I spend a lot of my time reflecting on what it means to be a community. It seems many people have stopped thinking about it. They have disengaged and are busy living active demanding lives. To keep community alive, we all need to contribute. The first Christian communities were not perfect nor were they saints but they stuck together even though they were struggling. They worked together sometimes under a veil of secrecy to create community and live compassionate lives.

The Church has always been the glue that kept communities together, beginning with the early Christian Church. It would be a mistake to idealize the early church as it too had its problems and internal struggles. This is not somewhere to which we should seek to return. They did, however, represent something different and although it attracted its oppressors and persecutors it had its devoted followers. These followers saw themselves as a body woven together by a bond of vocation and a common hope. This is lost to us, which is such a pity.

It is written that Christianity provided new norms and new kinds of social relationships. This seemed to be welcomed in what looked like an era of turmoil and unknowing. It offered charity as well as hope, so people wanted to be part of it. It provided a new sense of family with those who became dedicated followers.This is the kind of community to which I want to belong. The kind of community we can reimagine. The kind of community that is already there if only we could be open to it.

In the past, we gave too much clout to our clergy, to the individual in our communities. Very often this was an excuse on our behalf to opt-out.

Of course, many among the clergy enjoyed the influence they wielded. But that is in the past now. In 1959, Vatican II was announced by Pope John XXIII but it was 1962 before the first session was held. In all, sixteen documents were issued. The tide was turning for the Church and for traditional communities. People became excited to be part of something new. It was a Church for the modern era. Wouldn't it be great if we could become excited to be part of something new?

Wouldn't it be great if we could harness some of what we experienced as young children, for our youth? Take an example from Vatican II and become co-responsible for our communities? We went to Mass religiously in Broadford every Sunday. There was never a question of not going. Even as teenagers we all went. Admittedly, sometimes we went to be seen in our new coat or our new shoes. Sometimes we went for the chat afterwards. Sometimes we went to see our latest boy crush. But even in all of this we knelt and prayed and felt the sense of togetherness and community. My friends and I sang in the church choir. We were involved and were happy to be so.

It is no longer cool for young people to be involved in Church. Recently I travelled throughout Clare speaking at Masses and I was surprised over and over with the attendance in some churches. It is well known that there are fewer numbers than ever before going to weekend Masses. Going to Mass was once so strong in Irish life that it somehow defined us. However, in Ireland, we are losing our faith quicker than any other Western country.

The inevitable, although flagged was ignored and many hoped it would right itself. But this is not so. The days of our youth are gone. The family rosary is gone, young people going to Mass is gone.

Gradually, the traditional Irish Church is unravelling. How many remember the picture of the Sacred Heart with its light on your grandparent's wall? Usually, it was placed right next to John and Jackie Kennedy. Nonetheless, faith is still a strong part of Irish values and maybe we can reimagine our way forward.

After all, in the 2011 census, eighty-four per cent of the people of the Irish Republic described themselves as 'Roman Catholic'. Even though this fell in the 2016 census to seventy-eight per cent, it still demonstrates that the Catholic Church remains the majority religious body in Ireland. It is still important to people's lives. The actual practice is another thing. Country pilgrimages still flourish, and I would endeavour to say they are growing. People find them to be a spiritual experience. We are also wonderful when it comes to world disasters and times of need. This is an area where the community excels.

Even if the structures of the Church are weaker, some of the caring, sympathetic impulses of faith are still there. People are still actively seeking baptism, communion, confirmation and marriage and we all need our priest for our dead. How we do funerals is a mainstay of our tradition. It is a time of community out-pouring and a time when Churches are full, even if half those attending do not know when to kneel and when to stand. There is undoubtedly a difference from one Mass to another. This comes down not only to the individual priest but to how the community becomes involved.

Having attended more than a hundred and fifty Masses in the past year I experienced many different feelings; feelings of elation, feelings of sadness, feelings of joy, feelings of wonder, feelings of frustration but above all feelings of hope.

Hope in seeing communities coming together. We all know the saying where there is life there is hope, and there is definitely life even if it is somewhat exhausted.

We live in a time where what we do, where we live, what we earn, what we wear and our friendships, are all hugely important to us. It is all about achieving and reaching the top rather than fundamental values. I know many people look at others focusing on their outer appearance, defining them by what they do, how they look and what they earn rather than the inner values they possess.

I am delighted I see people for who they are deep down. I have never been interested in material things. I like to have a nice reliable car and a warm house with food in the fridge but to be honest, richness to me is peace of mind. This is hard to come by and it took me time to find.

It is good to experience the compassion and spirituality of our foundations. It is also important to stay in tune with our local surroundings and to stay involved with our local community. It is good for the mind, body, and soul. Many people say they are interested in spirituality but not in religion and this is understandable. There is a significant move away from the institutional Church and towards a more open spirituality. This is an area that needs to be acknowledged and discussed.

Creating spirituality in the community can be exciting. Our communities in Ireland have predominantly been Catholic up to now. These congregations tended to be staid and unchanging. But it doesn't have to be like this. As communities, we can be creative. We can be imaginative. We can reimagine. We do not need to wait for the local Church or clergy to introduce a retreat, a mission, a pilgrimage, a ritual.

We can initiate our own contribution. No need to wait for something you would like to see in your community, why not offer it yourself? It just matters that you are sharing your talents and are surrounded by comparatively open-minded people. In general, a sincere spiritual community will be focused on love, kindness, and inclusivity.

Making our communities more spiritual gives us space to be supportive of each other. There is no reason why we should not explore a new and experiential path.

Developing our deeper, inner knowing, can only benefit our communities. It is about creating space for you to get to know yourself and to get to know your communities. Finding support from a community that is spiritual can be very sustaining for all. People are amazing. They will help you to open your heart particularly when you have difficult moments. Spiritual communities are all about helping each other just like our communities of old in Ireland. Your support will also help and support them in their lives. With everyone open to giving and receiving support from each other we will soon begin to see new types of relationships forming within our communities.

Our tight-knit local communities can be laden with jealousy and resentment, and so many other harmful issues. Things will not be perfect. But we will have a better chance of working things out, creating more deep and powerful connections with others if we all become accepting. The core of our local communities stems from the passion of those living there. They desire social justice, equality, fairness, and inclusion for all. To create genuine, honest healthy communities we need to work together.

Our dedication to community here in Ireland did not appear out of nowhere. It comes from the values and principles that are derived from our backgrounds, our ancestors, our cultures as well as our experiences. These beliefs and traditions shape our vision of our community and the world. Our values and principles stemmed from our ancestors. We have deeply held beliefs about how the world should be. These beliefs are largely determined by religion, culture, and society. We have arrived at our values and principles through careful thought and reflection on life and experience.

The underpinnings of our understanding of community are derived from experience, experiment, and knowledge. In Ireland, there is a major devotion to local community. Where all of us long for equality and a reasonable quality of life for everyone living there. We have inherited a sacredness of life and an obligation to help, especially in times of need. This is something we all hold dear and take very seriously.

Our values are a reflection on the way each of us sees life. Our core belief is that everyone in our community has a right to a decent quality of life. The fundamentals are shelter, food, and income to support individuals and families. Everyone is worthy of understanding, respect, and equal consideration. This is something we cherish in Ireland. We all have hopes and dreams for our community and try to realise these dreams creatively. Many of us become so bogged down in concerns about the challenges ahead that we forget to breathe, think creatively, and allow it to work out when there is calm.

Values in the Community

Communities can be built by exploring the values we hold. Taking the time to consider our values with others takes us through many aspects and viewpoints. It is like learning a new language or like looking back at where we came from. Examining our culture and traditions can be hugely constructive when trying to move forward. In doing this we can discover our own values, and the bearing these values have on the environment. We build and model our community with our family and neighbours every day.

Maybe purposefully exploring values as a theme in a meeting, workshop or gathering could be a great way to get people involved. We can learn a lot from the values of others. Regardless of where we learn our values, the community provides a foundation for our growth as conscientious, caring people. Anyone who feels part of a community will support and uphold the values of the community, encouraging and promoting the well-being of its inhabitants. The more our community nurtures us and meets our needs, the more we feel attached to that community. The more values are lived out and practised the more the community will flourish.

Learning to meet the needs of those in our community helps us build a trusting, respectful relationship with all who live there. It helps us feel more invested and will help others feel the same. Perhaps we could challenge how our community functions if we are not happy. Become involved and help discover why the community operates the way it does and hear other people's opinions before complaining. Look at developing our own ideas and offering them to the community.

Reflect on what is happening in our community and give support. This allows full expression and avoids misunderstandings. Each community differs. Brainstorming within the community is a great way of forming a way forward. Reflecting on our cultural background, our prior lived experiences, our values, all add value to our community. Once we identify how our values shape our community, we can measure them against the values of others. Celebrate diversity and guard ourselves against narrow-mindedness which can be toxic. This may mean revising our values occasionally if we wish to engage everyone in the community. It is important that those volunteering within the community see the worth of the work they are doing.

Recognizing where our beliefs are rooted and how that moulds our thinking is of major importance to how we move forward. Everyone should have the opportunity to be involved in community decisions. Holding meetings or gatherings to arrive at some agreed changes is very healthy. Meeting the hopes and expectations of community can be an overriding goal. Learning how to resolve conflicts, how to make friends, how to listen to one another, how to control our behaviour and how to appreciate one another's perspectives can teach us how to live and work together as a community.

If we look to our ancestors, we will see that values are shown to be kindness and respect for all people, humility, honesty, generosity, self-control, and forgiveness. These values promote peace and goodwill. Those of us who strive for good may find peace of mind, a peace of heart, that no other rewards can match. Serving our community by sharing our values and striving to be good can reveal the real heart of the community.

We should not wait to be served but serve. By showing value in community, we can establish a secure, trusting place to live. Although morals and values are difficult to separate from each other we do not need to delve too deep as long as we are aware of our own values and our own morals and share them. Our moral code is formed by our family and our community.

Our very first community of influence is of course our family. Our behaviour is driven by the desire to be loyal to our upbringing. We adapt our morals with indicators from our family, from our friends and from the social groups to which we belong. We follow the prompts provided by our moral community on how to behave. Wherever we go in the world we remain connected to our community of origin.

This is evident by all those who emigrate but yearn for home. Reflecting on community we understand what we stand for and we never really leave it behind. Being part of the bigger picture helps us be happy, empowered, successful well-rounded individuals. By reinforcing each other we build confidence. With this shared reinforcement, we can take responsibility for our ethos and pass it on. In opening up to others and their experiences, we become equipped to rise to any occasion.

Communicating in a comfortable environment each person can take pride in expressing their own experiences and opinions while respecting others. This will make for sustainable communities.

The Community Man

While studying theology at Mary Immaculate College, Limerick, I studied 'The historical Jesus' a subject I loved. I struggle with my faith daily. One day I believe, the next I am full of questions. The one thing I am sure of though is that Jesus did exist. The evidence for Jesus of Nazareth has long been established. Within a few decades of his supposed lifetime, he is mentioned by several Jewish and Roman historians. He is also mentioned by dozens of Christian writers. There is both early and detailed testimony of His existence. Paul was the first of the Christian writers to talk about Jesus.

Those in the know agree that the earliest of these letters were written within twenty-five years of the death of Jesus. Other accounts of Jesus are in the New Testament gospels which were written around forty years after his death. To our knowledge the first author outside the church to mention Jesus is Flavius Josephus, a Jewish historian. Twenty years later we learn that Jesus was executed by Pontius Pilate from the high-ranking Roman politicians Tacitus and Pliny. Neither of them liked Christians so it is believed in mentioning Jesus they were telling the truth.

Jesus was denounced by Jewish Rabbis for being the illegitimate child of Mary and a sorcerer. Pagans dismissed Him as a scoundrel. None of them questioned whether Jesus lived. There were many stories about the birth, ministry, and death of Jesus over the centuries but few of them denied his existence. The overriding evidence is that the man Jesus did exist. He was a man of the community. He wanted everyone to be healthy and happy.

Whether we believe that Jesus was divine or not, we have to agree that he showed us how to live. Like so many of us now in this modern era Jesus never asked 'what is in this for me'. Jesus was driven by service. He took the time to hang out with everyone living His life as an example and backed up everything with His actions.

Jesus told us to 'Love one another, as I have loved you' (John 15:12) so when we love the world just as He loved it, we will find peace. That, for me, is what community is all about. Love. Once we begin to reach out to others who have not experienced love, we will experience a loving and fulfilled community. If we act out of love, we are more likely to live happily in harmony with each other.

Learning about the historical Jesus gave me a new understanding of how important our community involvement is. Reaching out to others will help us grow as people and will help us become spiritually mature.Jesus is a great source of enlightenment for all whether we believe in God or not.

Living as Jesus lived can only benefit ourselves, our families, and our communities. Jesus had a vision that the naked would be clothed, the blind would see, and the hungry would be fed. Most of us view this vision as Utopian. Jesus was an inspiration, a man of the community who attracted followers from all areas of society. By all accounts, He was a very charismatic man, a teacher, a healer and a storyteller. Jesus modelled a creative, empathetic, non-violent approach to everyone he met. Millions of people follow the examples of Jesus. During His life on earth, Jesus showed great love, compassion and understanding to everyone he met. He helped the poor, the rich, the outcast, and the sinners.

He taught us to reach out and help each other. He taught us to love.

As we show love for those in the community, we become more aware of self-worth, more enthusiastic about life, and more receptive to diversity. We can all live as Jesus did. Whether or not we choose to believe, whether or not we practice our faith, if we follow His example, we will allow ourselves to live a fulfilled life.

The Catholic Community

We need to remember that although Catholics are struggling here in Ireland, globally church membership is on the increase. But for this chapter, we will delve into Catholicism in Ireland with particular emphasis on the local community.

While speaking with local Parish Pastoral Councils throughout County Clare many topics were examined. There were questions and concerns and there was lethargy among many council members who felt dejected. This was to be expected. However, there was energy evident especially where lay people took an active interest in their Church and their faith community.

Born into a Catholic family in a Catholic community I am not even sure that I fully appreciate what that meant. My travels throughout the Killaloe Diocesan community affirmed for me that people love their Church and their community.

The press may hit out at it. Lapsed Catholics may scoff at it. Even those still practising may find fault with it, but there is a desire for the church to be a guiding light in the community.

Sometimes relationships become strained. There is a feeling of hopelessness out there, nonetheless, if a deeper look is taken, there are opportunities for change and change is needed. The big question is are we willing to change or would we prefer to sit back and complain. It is good to change and evolve, to grow and become better versions of ourselves so why not our Church?

One of my favourite movies, Shawshank Redemption, has a saying 'get busy living or get busy dying' so let's get busy living. Busy changing, busy evolving. Our environment changes, our culture changes, even we change, so why not the church. The question is, how does it change? Many would like to go back to an earlier version of Church, but it is never good to go back. Perhaps take lessons from the past, our past experiences but not return to the past. A simple restructuring will not do. Radical change is needed. There is a huge search in our present time for spirituality.

A new Church may be the key. It could be dynamic, it could be brave, it could be reasoned and above all, it could be inspiring. In activating change we need to be inspiring. Inspire others by the way we live. Inspire others to live their lives to their very fullest. Inspire people to inspire others.

In that way, we can have active inspirational communities. Change is crucial and inescapable. Let the life-giving spirit within create this change. Somewhere along the way, something went severely wrong. Somewhere we lost our means of communicating the value of a good, working, spiritual community.

It appears that we have failed in showing our youth how to live their best life. We became very focused on results and achievements.

We suddenly became the sum of our achievements instead of the person we are. This in turn has put huge pressure on our young people to do well rather than to be well. We all need to change. We need to become the change our community needs.

Change is difficult. My daughter once told me that it takes twenty-one days to change a bad habit when I was trying to give up sugar. I do not know where she got this statistic from, but it did not work for me. Loving chocolate is so deeply ingrained in my lifestyle that it is difficult to change. I failed many times before finally coming to terms with my craving for chocolate. This may be a simplified way of looking at it but effective, nonetheless.

Patience is needed while implementing change as it is made up of wonderfully flawed human beings. Change will come slowly. It will come as we grow and become fulfilled happy human beings. It will come as we begin to live our own true lives. In becoming better human beings our communities will become better places also.

In becoming more spiritual, more inspiring our mission and vocation will be fulfilled. When we blossom, our communities will blossom. We can begin immediately to develop whatever is necessary to engage everyone in the community. From tradition, we learned about love and compassion. We show our compassion in the way we raise our children, the way we relate to our friends, our extended family, our neighbours, and our co-workers.

Our communities were founded on the principles of togetherness. Let us help this to continue. Although the Mass was the central celebration within our communities, our modern life is more fully lived away from the Church building.

Tradition dictates we serve one another, we are called to take care of the poor, to take care of our environment and to ensure justice and integrity for all. We do not need a Church building to do this.

Family 'love one another' My aunt Kitty to the left Mam to the right me in the middle

Chapter Five

Structures: Parish and Diocese

I don't think that scheduling is uncreative. I
think that structure is required for creativity.
Twyla Tharp

Our Parish

Most of us here In Ireland, readily identify ourselves with our Parish community. In general, it is how our schools and religious systems are structured and organised. Wherever we go in the world we habitually refer to our parish community as our foundation. Civil parishes are the administrative units of the state. There are about 2,500 civil parishes in Ireland. In this book, we refer mostly to the Ecclesiastical or Church parish. This parish type has been in existence in Ireland for many years. Indeed, the civil parish boundaries followed those established by the Church.

Sometimes Roman Catholic and Civil Parish are the same, however, this is not always the case. Catholic and civil parishes both grew from the initial mediaeval parishes. In 1829 Catholic Emancipation produced a Devotional Revolution which created a great upsurge in the number of priests, in turn allowing for smaller parishes. Now with the collapse in religious vocations, this may be reversed.

In Catholic parishes throughout Ireland, the parish council looked after the running of the parish. Its purpose is to witness and share the good news of Jesus. It encourages parishioners to get involved with the wider community and provide care for the vulnerable in their community. The parish council became the parish pastoral council in the aftermath of Vatican II. We here in Ireland have only embraced the Parish Pastoral Council in recent years. Many are still coming to terms with what it means to be pastoral. Parish pastoral growth happens when priests and people work together, in an environment of mutual appreciation and respect.

It is a local leadership group that is informed by the wider diocesan community.

The Parish Pastoral Council

Although there is a commitment of lay men and women who have a desire to be active in the pastoral structures of their community and their diocese, there is still a long way to go. There are outstanding Parish Pastoral Councils who are looking to the future. They are shaping a way forward by being creative and inspirational. It is heartening to see how they are enriching their ministry.

On the other hand, there are also Pastoral Councils who have not yet grown in their task as they are unsure of their role. Then some Pastoral Councils are being held back as they are under the thumb of their priest. While completing workshops in the Diocese of Killaloe, the fostering of the participation of lay men and women was encouraged. Any priest who does not welcome this does not have the best interest of his community in mind. We all need to show our love of humanity through our love for each other and our community.

Setting targets as Pastoral Councils is a healthy way forward. With everyone working together we can look to renewal and revitalisation. We need to look to ongoing formation in faith as well as in structure not only for Pastoral Councils but for the community at large. Commitment to the people in our community is paramount as is responding to the challenging situations ahead. Reforming how we think and how we do things requires the ability to look afresh at the fundamentals of our communities and how we can live in the challenging conditions of our time.

It takes time and effort to become involved in your community. People have too little time to spare these days. There is no point in thinking that we can go back to the way things were. We cannot. Things have changed radically, and we are not tackling all the aspects of that change.

Parish Pastoral Councils now have the opportunity to focus on reshaping our way forward. We live in a particular time in a particular culture. The life of our community is formed by that culture. It is up to us to influence and mould our culture and philosophy so we can become sustainable communities into the future.

The main responsibility for ensuring our Church and our communities survive into the future belongs to Parish Pastoral Councils. The lay men and women who participate in Pastoral Councils live and work in the outside world. They have the appropriate skills and knowledge required to sustain our communities into the future. Difficult questions need to be asked. Questions about the community, about the family, about marriage and sexuality. Make our communities more inclusive.

The Christian message is important to the growth of our communities, it would be good to protect and transmit it. Participants of Pastoral Councils have a responsibility to share their values by how they live their own lives within the community.

In recognizing the failings and betrayal of the past it would be good to reimagine our way forward. We could look to renewal. Turn back to Jesus and his example to form communities like those of the early Church. They were devoted to fellowship and the breaking of bread with each other.

Sharing goodwill with the community with kind and open hearts would enrich the lives of all. See change as an opportunity. Take it as a challenge to deepen relationships. The community of tomorrow will be made stronger by the journey upon which we are embarking. Now is the time for exploration.

Reimaging the way forward should not be because of the decline in vocations. We need to see the challenges as an invitation to create new relationships within the community. Embrace Vatican II all over again. Explore the vision of the Church presented to us as 'the people of God'. Generate new bonds with all those around us.

The work in the Diocese of Killaloe has a lot of positive things happening. Despite this, many Pastoral Councils are tired. They need opportunities to help them enrich their role. Communities are still alive, but can we ensure they stay that way as many are already on life support. Many Pastoral Councils have been stuck. Stuck in the maintenance role. Perhaps now we need to look at deepening the roles of those actively involved in the community. It is a learning curve. We can all learn from one another. In coming together, we can really make it work.

The contributions of Parish Pastoral Councils have been truly significant. They are responsible for the change and renewal that have taken place so far. They have been through the traumas of the past and have hung in there with hope for the future. Together with the clergy, they took on the responsibility to resolve the crisis which they did not cause. Lay men and women gently supported child safeguarding to ensure a safe future for generations to come. Communities are richer due to the contributions made by Pastoral Councils. It is now time to show appreciation for their valued contributions throughout the years.

We could look at how we can help them develop and become sustainable into the future. Because without effective, mature Pastoral Councils, a community will struggle. Taking part in the monthly meeting to reflect on the future would be a step in the right direction.

Each council is unique in how it operates but it would be good to have some structure. Setting time aside for reflection is what differentiates the Pastoral Council from the Parish Council. There is an ongoing need for Councils to avail of training. This is something the Diocese should provide. Embarking on a genuine platform of contemplation, reflection and formation will ensure the future of Pastoral Councils. We referred to the maintenance and mission debate earlier in this book. Above all, Pastoral Councils need to be in 'missionary mode'.

This can be difficult for many as they feel awkward. Maintenance is easy. Fixing things is easy. Mission on the other hand can be difficult. But it is necessary for the health of our communities into the future. We need to reach out to our young, to our elderly, to our vulnerable. We need programmes that foster faith formation.

We need to demonstrate a caring presence within the community. The Parish Pastoral Council of the future could reach out to those on the margins of our society. They could listen to what is being said and try within their own remit to respond to the demands of modern life.

The Parish Pastoral Council could be the channel to safeguarding a new vision. We are all in service to each other and our communities. Creating a sense of belonging is the ultimate goal. A sense of belonging in the community. It is not about the building, but the people.

Our Church buildings were denied to us before here in Ireland, but the 'Church' continued as faithful communities still found a way of getting together. Maybe it is time we revised the Mass Rock. Just a suggestion. We should at least look at ways of creating a different but enriching experience.

We cannot be an inward-looking Church or an inward-looking Pastoral Council. We cannot be just focused on our own concerns. We should rise above our self-centeredness and look outward to encounter the love in our communities.

Sometimes we get bogged down in internal politics, but we can look beyond this. This can be difficult where there are ongoing issues within Pastoral Councils but if we let go of our own prejudices for the greater good, we will benefit greatly. I firmly believe we can become excited as Pastoral Councils. After all, you are now shaping what the future will look like. Ask yourselves 'what would you like your community to look like in ten years?'

I know what I would like. I would like vibrant, committed, passionate communities that look after and love one another. Communities of outreach. Communities of joy. Pope Francis tells us that 'Life grows by being given away and it weakens in isolation and comfort. Those who enjoy life most are those who leave security on the shore and become excited by the mission of communicated life to others'. So, let's become excited about our mission.

Parish Pastoral Councils are strategically placed to think actively about how to cope with our present reality. The reality is the declining number of priests. A recent report commissioned by the Dublin Diocese predicted a drop of between sixty-one per cent and seventy per cent in the number of priests in ministry by 2030.

This will no doubt be replicated throughout the Island of Ireland. The stark statistics tell us that we are fast approaching a time when a priest leaves a parish he will not be replaced. As priests retire, become ill or are transferred there is no other priest to replace them. This means that there will be many parishes without a resident priest.

As this book is written, in the Diocese of Killaloe there are thirteen parishes without a resident priest. Most of these parishes did not have time to prepare. It came as a shock to them. Nonetheless, they gathered together and planned for their future. Some of these Pastoral Councils are now very strong as a result. We come back once more to the question 'what would you do as a Pastoral Council if you did not have a priest?' This is a question that needs to find some answers.

Since Vatican II there has been a greater involvement of lay people with Ministers of the Word, Ministers of the Eucharistic, members of Parish Pastoral Councils, Parish Finance Committees, Ushers, Altar Servers, Safeguarding, Eucharistic Adoration groups, sacramental preparation teams and choirs. There are also many positive parish initiatives. We should appreciate all these people and provide them with the resources they need. It is so important to nourish those who are offering their time in the service of the whole community.

Some of us can remember a time when there were two or three priests to a parish. Now we have one if we are lucky. Sharing the responsibilities of the community is the way forward. Every diocese, every parish, indeed every local Church is being impacted. Consideration needs to be given to enabling pastoral care to continue within the community.

Greater involvement of Parish Pastoral Councils and parishioners is a positive step forward. The future will greatly differ from the past in terms of how we are as faith communities.

Putting new structures in place aiming to strongly support a new vision of pastoral leadership with priests and lay leaders ministering together is now essential. We need to remember how important it is to help people understand the changes that are coming down the road. For many, the change will not be easy, but with our example, the rewards of genuine collaborative leadership will be recognized as good for all. For example, collaborative support will benefit the community greatly. Better decisions will be made from the collective wisdom of all involved. As Pastoral Councils become more missionary focused, the community will flourish.

Parishioners will be better served because the community will be able to draw on the gifts, talents, and skills of all. As Parish Pastoral Councils work alongside their clergy and other parish teams, they deepen their understanding and practice of being co-responsible. Having Pastoral Workers available to facilitate leadership teams and parish groups with pastoral planning, evaluation, formation of mission statements, and pastoral council formation would be a great advantage.

Guidelines for Pastoral Councils

Each Pastoral Council should have their own framework, taking into account the particular needs of its parish. This framework should help each parish put together their own guidelines. The guidelines should remain faithful to the basic nature of Parish Pastoral Councils defined in the documents of Vatican II. Reviewing the guidelines regularly is highly recommended.

Parish Pastoral Councils are leadership structures that make it possible for priests and people to work together. Building dynamic Christian communities into the future is no longer an easy task. All the skills, gifts and talents of the priest and the Parish Pastoral Council must be called upon to evangelize and reach out to the entire community. It is down to them to discover what is best for their community. This should involve the whole community in a response that would make for more inclusivity.

Making structures available and putting the needs of the parish to the fore is paramount. Compiling lists of people willing to offer their skills in certain areas would be a great idea. Having a bank of different skills and talents available to the community could prove invaluable.

I once heard of a community that asked its members to donate a few hours of their expertise to their community. Others in the community could then draw from this expertise when it was needed. I felt this was a great idea. For instance, a local solicitor could donate three hours to the skill bank. If a painter needed a solicitor, he could use their service and he would then donate his skill to the community bank where someone could draw upon it when they are in need. This would involve great organization to set up and would be difficult to get people to invest their time, but it would be an amazing benefit to the community as well as bring people together.

Communication is very important when it comes to Pastoral Councils. There is no point in meeting month after month discussing the needs of the community if the community do not know what you are doing. A community must know who their representatives are so if they have concerns, they can approach you. Therefore, communicating what you do, who you are and where people can contact you is important. Having an effective dialogue between concerned groups within the community can only lead to becoming more inclusive.

A Pastoral Council should review its workings on an ongoing basis. Evaluating what is happening locally and reading the signs of the times should be mandatory. It is constructive to reassess the life and activities of the community from time to time so that parishioners might have a sense that their Pastoral Council and their priest is working in their best interest.

Membership

Two of the questions I am often asked are, who our members should be and how do we select them? This is certainly down to each community. In general, members should be able to commit to attending at least two-thirds of meetings throughout the year. They should also be available to participate in Pastoral Council events.

When it comes to selecting members, communities should agree on a process that is suitable to their own particular area and situation. Some of the options I encountered as a Pastoral Worker are as follows;

- Election by the parish community
- Nomination by parishioners
- Selection of representatives from other parish organisations
- Selection by the parish priest in consultation with the present council
- Where there is difficulty forming a Council people are asked directly

Members of Pastoral Councils should be representative of all in the community. They should concentrate on what is best for the wider community and not the individual. It is all about becoming co-responsible. Members normally serve no more than two terms. These terms are normally decided beforehand and in general, are either three years or five years. Usually, the term of membership is three years as it is difficult to get people to serve for longer.

This is something that needs to be decided in advance as people should know what they are signing up to. It may be possible for a member to be re-elected if they are willing. Sometimes casual vacancies arise. If this happens it is down to the existing Pastoral Council members themselves to may fill this vacancy by invitation. Another query that often arises in connection with Pastoral Councils is how many members they should have. Again, this is subjective.

Normally for a meeting to run and act well, it should consist of between twelve and fifteen members. This is down to the community and its size.

After a Parish Pastoral Council comes together it needs to decide on its officers. These are usually proposed and seconded by those present. In some instances, members are elected. In general, there are four officer positions. The president, the chairperson, the secretary, and the diocesan representative. Some Pastoral Councils also have an assistant secretary and a communications officer.

More often than not the parish priest is the president. If there is no resident priest, the priest in charge of administering the parish would sit in when time allowed. Together with the chairperson, they convene the meetings.

The chairperson is elected by the members of the council. They will serve for a pre-determined period. The role of the chairperson is convening the meetings together with the president or in some cases the secretary. They prepare the agenda with the secretary, and they facilitate the meetings. A chairperson might wish to appoint a vice-chairperson to assist or to chair the meeting when they are not available.

The position of secretary is a busy one. They are responsible for keeping minutes. They circulate the minutes as much as possible before the meeting. They also circulate relevant material to the council members. Sometimes an assistant secretary is also elected to help with the administration and to take notes when the secretary is absent.

Sometimes there is a cluster or diocesan contact person. This is a position new to a lot of councils. They generally liaise between the parish, the pastoral area, and the diocese through the appropriate diocesan representative.

If there is a communications person, they will take care of all communications. Notices to newspapers, posters for upcoming events, interviews if required. The responsibilities of the Pastoral Council members will differ according to the needs of each community.

As a rule, however, they will be required to;
- Attend the meetings regularly. Never missing three in a row.
- Contribute to the discussions, debates and considerations of the council.
- Support the implementation of council policies wherever possible.
- Take part in any training provided.
- Take advantage of ongoing formation.

The guidelines of the Parish Pastoral Council should state how often meetings are held. Some councils may need to meet monthly. Other councils may choose less frequent meetings. Most Pastoral Councils meet once a month taking the summer months off. The minimum requirement for meetings is generally five times a year. There must be a good relationship between those in the Parish Pastoral Council.

It is central to each stage of the decision-making process. Respect is paramount as is considering the talents, skills and expertise of the members. Pastoral Councils should clarify the minimum number of members who should attend the meeting before it is deemed an official meeting. Generally, the minimum number required is one over one half. The Pastoral Council is mainly involved with encouraging action through pastoral planning.

This may sometimes comprise of setting up occasional committees to take on once-off projects. Each Diocese is committed to making resources available. They will assist with ongoing training and formation at all levels. The financial well-being of the Parish is generally catered for by the Finance Committee which may or may not include Pastoral Council members.

Parish Pastoral Council – initiatives

From visiting Parish Pastoral Councils, it came to light they were never sure if they were doing the right thing. Many of them felt tired and were unaware of how much they were actually doing. Being a Pastoral Council does not mean being a project manager, nor is it just about the organization of events. But events are important in bringing the community together whether it is a small or large gathering. We need to change the mindset of being focused on numbers and make it a wonderful experience no matter how many attend. Pastoral Councils were always looking for inspiration. Among the initiatives promoted by the Parish Pastoral Councils I met are as follows:

- Formulating a parish Mission Statement.
- Setting up a Friendly Call service for housebound parishioners to ensure they are contacted by telephone every day.
- Establishing an Active Retirement Group - to provide an outlet for parishioners of more mature years.
- Developing Parish Websites – facilitating communication.
- Providing speakers on a diversity of life experiences.

- Seeking ways to create a more welcoming parish – ie: a communications board in Church porch.
- Organising Area Masses for the various parts of the parish including graveyard masses.
- Developing a Child Protection Policy and Child Protection -Guidelines for the parish in collaboration with the parish's Child Protection Officers.
- Providing training in child protection and facilitating Garda vetting for people whose involvement in the parish could bring them into contact with children.
- Organising an annual 'Volunteering Day' to make parishioners aware of opportunities to become involved in the various groups serving the community.
- Producing the Parish Newsletter.
- Conducting Parish Surveys.
- Organising a Parish Mission/Retreat.
- Bringing together parish groups and ministries.
- Set up Social Justice groups
- Set up hospitality Groups.
- Facilitate Youth Masses.
- Provide links with schools etc.
- Pilgrim Walks.
- Provide ongoing upskilling and workshops.
- Provide Music workshops.
- Christmas: children's liturgy.
- Play and pray groups.
- Lenten scripture reflections.
- Triduum: Holy Thursday stations of the cross and prayer around the cross.

- Celebrating the liturgy for St Brigid's Day – a demonstration on how to make the St Brigid's Cross.
- Organizing parish novena.
- Special liturgy of renewal and healing for the sick.
- Establish a sacred space.
- Provide commentaries for certain feasts and celebrations.
- Resources for music ministry groups.
- Mass aimed at those who are housebound or are ill or in hospital.
- Defibrillator. Train people to use the defibrillator.
- School art and Essay competitions.
- Parish social – a way for the Parish to thank all the people who give so much of their time in different ways.

The groups represented included the following:
- Ministers of the Eucharist
- Ministers of the Word
- Church Cleaner Teams
- Altar Group· Flowers
- Collectors/Counters both at Mass and Door to Door
- Do this in Memory Team
- Confirmation Teams
- Baptism Group
- Bereavement Group
- Altar Servers Trainers
- Altar servers
- All others with a role in the community

Volunteering in Parish Pastoral Councils can sometimes leave you feeling tired, frustrated even exasperated. It can be discouraging but sometimes we need to 'put out into the deep water and lower our nets for a catch.' Over and over in the life of the Pastoral Council, we are challenged. It is at times like this that we need to search deeper and further for solutions. This can be difficult. The trick is to be daring in trying new things.

Sometimes we need to look for what businesspeople call a 'game-changer.' As a society, we have fallen out of love with 'Mass' I can understand why. The Mass prayers should uncover God's vision for us. It should remind us that we are pilgrims on a journey through life but most now no longer attend or tune out.

Recently I came to the realisation that prayer can be a great way of meditating. Truly listening to prayer can help fulfil spiritual needs. Pastoral councils should have a reflection that means something to them as a group and have hope.

The Diocese of Killaloe – my experience

The Diocese of Killaloe is a Roman Catholic diocese in mid-western Ireland established in the seventh century and comprises parts of the counties of Clare, Tipperary, Offaly, Limerick, and Laois. It is part of the ecclesiastical province of Cashel. It is one of the larger dioceses in the country, with the Catholic population estimated at 120,000 persons. When St. Flanann was consecrated as the successor of St. Lua or Molua as Bishop in 639 it is said that the diocese was established. The boundaries of the Diocese of Killaloe as we know them today were largely established at that time.

162

Some changes were made throughout the centuries as referred to at the Synod of Kells when the Diocese of Roscrea was made part of the Diocese of Killaloe. Also referred to at the Synod of Kells is the Diocese of Scattery Island which became part of Killaloe during the twelfth century.

St. Flannan, mentioned above, was the son of Theodoric the seventh-century king of Thomond. He was described as a truly Christian king, a missionary rather than a ruler of a kingdom. He openly professed his faith. St. Flannan studied his faith and scripture under the guidance of St. Blathmet and later under St. Molua. He was known to be an attentive and admirable student which meant he went on to succeed St. Molua as abbot. The local people as well as the clergy and bishops persuaded St. Flannan to accept the position of bishop. It is said he was reluctant at first but understood it was his calling. Subsequently, he set out for Rome and was ordained Bishop of Killaloe by Pope John IV (640-642).

Following his travels, St. Flannan discovered how people practised and followed their faith on the continent. He returned to Killaloe and made his jubilant people even more enlightened. He was known to be an excellent preacher as well as a caring man. He is also said to have performed many miracles. He believed in the importance of human justice and asked his people to encourage peace. To this day he is remembered in Killaloe where St. Flannan`s Oratory, The Roman Catholic church and the Cathedral is named in his honour.

The Diocese of Killaloe is one of six dioceses under the ecclesiastical province of Cashel. The cathedral church is situated in Ennis in County Clare. The bishop at present is Bishop Fintan Monahan.

I had the pleasure to work with Bishop Fintan and found him to be a very pleasant and caring man. He is very interested in seeing the Diocese thrive into the future. Bishop Fintan is a people's person and gets out to meet people as much as possible. He is also probably one of the fittest Bishops in the country. I have known him to run up Croagh Patrick, say Mass and run down again. Not an easy feat.

The Diocese today comprises fifty-eight parishes with about 100 priests working and ministering to the people and communities of the region. I was lucky to work with these priests especially those most interested in finding new ways forward. There were those, however, who resisted listening to the people and would prefer if the church remained clerical. They were afraid to let go of the reins as it meant losing power. Many people I met felt that the way forward would not be clear until these priests were gone. Thankfully, most priests were happy to welcome any assistance from the laity.

My visits as Pastoral Worker were always welcoming. Each pastoral area including each parish underwent three workshops. I facilitated these workshops, but the attendees were the driving force. I was amazed by the hunger that was out there for change and embracing that change. My experiences throughout were different and touching. I was touched by the areas I visited as well as the people I met. There are extraordinary people everywhere and I was lucky to meet them.

As mentioned above, the Diocese of Killaloe has fifty-eight parishes now divided into fifteen pastoral areas.

- Cois Fharraige – Cross, Carraigaholt, Kilkee and Doonbeg
- Inis Cathaigh – Kilrush, Killamer, Cooraclare, Kilmihil
- Radharc na n'Oileann – Kilmurry McMahon, Coolmeen, Lissycasey-Ballynacally
- Criocna Callan – Mullagh, Miltown-Malbay, Inagh, Kilmaley
- Abbey – Ennis, Doora-Barefield, Quin, Clarecastle
- Tradaree – Newmarket on Fergus, Shannon, Sixmilebridge
- Ceantar na Lochanna – Tulla, O'Callaghans Mills, Broadford
- Imeall Boirne – Tubber, Corofin, Ruan, Crusheen
- Inis Cealtra – Killeana, Feakle, Scariff, Mountshannon, Bodyke, Ogonnalloe
- Scath na Sionnaine – Killaloe, Clonlara, Castleconnell
- Odhran – Portroe, Youghalarra, Puckane, Nenagh, Silvermines, Templederry
- Ollatrim – Cloughjordan, Dunkerrin, Toomevara
- Cois Deirge – Terryglass, Borrisokane, Lorrha
- Brendan – Birr, Shinrone, Kilcolman, Kinnity
- Cronan – Roscrea, Bournea, Kyle, Knock (there may have been changes)

1. *Cois Fharraige*
2. *Inis Cathaigh*
3. *Radharc na nOileann*
4. *Criocha Callan*
5. *Abbey*
6. *Tradaree*
7. *Ceantar na Lochanna (my Broadford)*
8. *Imeall Boirne*
9. *Inis Cealtra*
10. *Scath na Sionnaine (My Killaloe)*
11. *Odhran*
12. *Ollatrim*
13. *Cois Deirge*

In the year prior to the publication of this book, the Killaloe diocesan appointments continued with the repeated curve of recent years with fewer and fewer priests available. They now have well over one-third of the fifty-eight parishes in the diocese without a resident priest under the age of seventy-five. Some priests have opted to continue ministering beyond the retirement age but they will not be able to continue this forever.

A different approach is needed now. Hope is needed. There is however a sign of hope for the diocese of Killaloe as there are twenty-five lay people trained in Pastoral Care and Catechetics. They are about to graduate. They will bring their talents to their Pastoral areas in the years to come. They will make a difference. Following on from the previous cluster area practice which had been in place for some years, new and current pastoral areas, as well as a Co-PP system came into effect in 2018. The intention is to relaunch this system.

I was one of two pastoral workers who facilitated a variety of pastoral and parish assemblies while implementing the leadership and partnership initiative of the pastoral plan. It was a time of learning and understanding for me. I can only hope I brought some awareness of leadership and partnership to the area gatherings.

In the past, the parish was mainly about prayer and the life in the parish revolved around the sacraments and Mass. While visiting the parishes of the diocese, new ways of living life and faith were explored. I have special memories from my time there.

My first gathering was in Kilrush where I met with the parishes of Cross, Carraigaholt, Kilkee, Doonbeg, Kilrush, Killamer, Knock, Cooraclare, Kilmihil.

I remember it well and I can now admit that although I appeared confident, I was very nervous. I knew I was the new kid on the block and everything I said and did would be scrutinized. Public speaking and giving presentations were familiar to me so I was confident in that respect. However, I was presenting to approximately 120 people and not all of them would agree with what I had to say. More than anything I did not want to upset anyone.

There were people there who would not embrace the new pastoral plan. As I said, I am confident with public speaking, but this was different. Although I am a deeply spiritual person, I am not comfortable sharing my soul with large groups. On that night I thought I would begin with a simple meditation to invite people to be present in the room and to leave their busyness outside. As I began, I saw some of the men at the back throwing their eyes heavenwards, so I was thrown off my stride. I am sure they thought I had taken leave of my senses. Nonetheless, we continued and I was thrilled with the response.

It was a lovely gathering of local communities. They all learned from each other and agreed they should meet like this more often. Subsequently, I returned to Kilrush several times and although I found some resistance in this area, I was invited to visit the parishes individually and was made to feel very welcome.

In Cooraclare, I was delighted to find a Pastoral Council in deep discussion on their way forward. Some were hesitant but soon I observed they were supportive of each other, and they decided to try some new forms of outreach. On the night I visited Doonbeg, I was lucky to meet with Fr Joe Haugh the priest famous for meeting Donald Trump.

I mention him because I totally judged the book by the cover and decided he would not be interested in anything I had to say. I felt he was old school. I was so wrong. Fr Joe was a well-respected man, adored by his congregation. On the night I met him, he mentioned a book to me on Jesus and who he was. He later posted that book to me which blew me away. This gesture meant so much, I felt accepted, and I have to say the book still means a lot to me.

I went on to meet with the Radharc na n'Oileann pastoral area which included Kilmurry McMahon, Coolmeen, Lissycasey-Ballynacally, Labasheeda, Kildysart. Here I was also invited to meet with each parish council individually and I was delighted with my reception. There is genuine joy in this area. The dedication the people here have to their communities was impressive. I had a Fr Ted experience in Coolmeen where it was insisted I had tea. Yes, the saying 'go on, go on, go on' and some lovely tart and cake I learned this was where the real meeting took place. After the structure of a meeting, the offering of a cup of tea helped people relax and they were happy to share their experiences and thoughts.

My visit to Lissycasey-Ballynacally was my first introduction to play-and-pray at Mass in Lissycasey church. It was simply beautiful. The children were so enthralling with their pictures and colouring. You could see their interest was held and they enjoyed the experience. In Kiladysart, I met with some of the most passionate people a community could have. They were very proactive.

I will always remember the energy in the room and the whole-hearted reception I received. This can also be said of Kilmurry-McMahon and Labasheeda. Although I will always remember Labasheeda as the only parish that did not applaud when I spoke at their Mass. I found it difficult stepping off that altar.

Meeting with the pastoral area of Criocna Callan – Mullagh, Quilty, Miltown-Malbay, Inagh, Kilmaley was also a memorable experience for me. To say I fell in love with this area is an understatement. The people here are blessed with the priests they have. I was so lucky to have a one-on-one with all of them and was so impressed with the love and loyalty of each one to their community. Because I live in Killaloe, I had a long drive every time I visited but I enjoyed the drive up and I always returned home feeling joy. The pastoral councils here listened and provided opportunities to the community to rediscover their worship whether inside the church building or outside.

In Miltown-Malbay I met a priest who blew me away with his insight and openness to discussion even though I had never met him at Diocesan gatherings. I met with confirmation children who entered into a retreat with trepidation but ended in faith and fun.

In Mullagh I met with a group of people who will forever hold a place in my heart. In Inagh/Kilnamona I was taken aback at how receptive they were to new ideas and how quickly they brought talk into action. Here also I found the oratory of The Blessed Mary Ever-Virgin. It is one of those places you enter and are immediately struck by the history and the feeling of inner peace. All churches have their uniqueness but some buildings you enter are more than buildings.
They fill you with peace and tranquillity and the oratory of The Blessed Mary Ever-Virgin was that to me. I continue to visit it to this day.

Another such church in this area was that of Our Lady of the Sea, Quilty.

It is situated in one of the most beautiful
vistas you are ever likely to see but it is when you go
inside it takes your breath away. For me, the history
of this church is seeped into the walls as it exudes
peace.

Blessed Mary Ever-Virgin (photo Kerry Blake)

Our Lady of the Sea, Quilty (Photo Kerry Blake)

In the parish of Kilmaley which included Inch and
Connolly, I encountered some of the most dedicated
people you are ever likely to meet. The people here
were already providing several lay activities. The
priests were highlt respect and supported.

Supporting the pastoral council in Clarecastle
was a joy for me. Here I was in contact with Fr Pat
Malone.

Fr Pat was chaplain to my children going to school and he is always remembered fondly in my community of Killaloe/Ballina. He was lucky now to be in the parish of Clarecastle/Ballyea. They were so community-minded, so proud of their traditions and they showed this by contributing their skills and talent.

Doora-Barefield was my first experience of Taize. I heard of it of course but never experienced it. To this day I find it to be such a peaceful way to be. Peacefully sitting together, sharing that sacred space a few precious moments of silence and then heading back to our busy lives may be a little better off for having shared the time in peace and tranquillity.

I met with the Tradaree pastoral area of Newmarket-on-Fergus, Shannon, Sixmilebridge in Shannon. Another night of learning for me. These parishes had amazing priests and as such had excellent support from their communities. I know Fr Arnie and Fr Tom won't mind if I single out Canon Brendan. I was always respectful of the older members of the clergy when I met them as I felt they may not understand the changes we were proposing. Canon Brendan was immediately welcoming, and he illuminated goodness from his every pore.

I also met Fr Harry here. His reputation of community preceded him. I read articles and books written by him and find his concepts around community to be praiseworthy. As with other pastoral areas each parish invited me to visit with them and all parishes here were enthusiastic and very supportive of each other. Fr Tom in Newmarket on Fergus was surrounded by excellent collaborators as were the other priests in this area.

When I met with Scath na Sionnaine consisting of Killaloe, Clonlara, Castleconnell and Ceantar na Lochanna to include Tulla, O'Callaghans Mills, Broadford it was like returning home. Coming from Broadford, going to school in Tulla and living in Killaloe, the first meeting could have been very daunting for me. But people were very kind and again, welcoming. This night presented a fun experience catching up with people with whom I was familiar. I knew Fr James in Killaloe from Mass – he was my parish priest. Fr Greed was familiar as I had so many relatives in Clonlara. Fr John I knew from Broadford and although I knew of the priests in Castleconnell I had never met them. Meeting them now was a revelation they were beyond welcoming and grateful for my support and me for theirs.

Meeting with the pastoral area of Imeall Boirne including the parishes of Tubber, Corofin, Ruan and Crusheen was the greatest eye-opener for me. This was the first area to pilot a cluster of parishes coming together. It was not hard to see how they could be used as an example to the other pastoral areas. They were creative and innovative in their ways of reaching out. They had a committed pastoral council and their leadership through their priests was notable. There was a warmth, a welcome and a sense of belonging in this area. They were connected and it was a joy to see. The way they participated in coming together communicated hospitality and inclusion to all.

I was also lucky to visit with the pastoral areas linked with my colleague Lorina. She had responsibility for the pastoral areas South of the Shannon, Odhran, Ollatrim, Cois Deirge, Brendan and Cronan. Lorina introduced everyone to a beautiful reflection called St Patrick's Breastplate, something I went on to use in the future.

As previously mentioned, I first worked under the guidance of Bishop Kieran O'Reilly. Kieran is a gentleman. Intelligent, academic, and above all caring to the world around him. He is a man of extreme faith and belief. My greatest memory of Kieran is that he was comfortable in any setting and inclusive of all. This is not to say he was not immune to controversy. At one time he hoped to introduce deacons, but this decision was put aside until it could be given more thought as it caused so much upset. To my knowledge, it was shelved completely, disappointing for those genuinely interested. I hope they will live out their calling in other ways.

Bishop Kieran went on to become Archbishop of Cashel and Emly, and I went on to work with the new Bishop of Killaloe, Bishop Fintan Monahan. He was very supportive of the Builders of Hope pastoral plan and helped in bringing it to its conclusion. I was disappointed to finish this project. I can only hope I left the diocese understanding what leadership and partnership meant to communities into the future.

I for one grew immensely while working there. I will always hold the clergy and people I met in my heart. I grew spiritually, morally, and emotionally. There was jealousy within the echelons of the church, and I was exposed to this more than once, but even though it felt isolating at the time I knew people were trying to cope with new ways of seeing things. They felt they were working in the best interest of their community.

When the Diocese of Killaloe introduced their Builders of Hope Plan it was creative and innovative. Those of us involved from the beginning were very excited by it.

In 2011, Bishop Kieran O'Reilly invited the people of Killaloe Diocese to engage in a listening process. Gatherings took place across the diocese with both clergy and lay representatives. Each parish took the opportunity to share their concerns and to begin a plan-for-the-future. Taking on board what people had to say was the basis for Builders of Hope.

It put forward a workable vision for Pastoral Development in the Diocese. This plan recognised the gifts of all and encouraged them to contribute to their parish, pastoral area, and diocese. I was appointed to work on the leadership and partnership areas of this plan. I was excited by the prospect as I believed in it. The way I saw it, we were planning for a reality where lay people would share responsibility with the clergy. We also hoped to support the personal and spiritual growth of all in the diocese.

Builders of Hope came into being at a time of great change for the Church. It would challenge us to make significant changes in our thinking and practice. Increasingly we live in a more material and pluralist society. It is difficult for the Church to find its role and voice in these times. Throughout our past, we depended on our priests to be leaders. However, now with the reduced number of priests, we need to look at how our local communities will be sustained into the future?

As previously noted, there are 137 Christian communities in the diocese of Killaloe. How these communities will be sustained into the future requires serious reflection and conversation. This is what the pastoral plan was all about. This plan would ask every member of the community to exercise a more active role in the community. My role in the plan was to help people prepare for a changing situation.

To help people recognise the declining numbers of the clergy was already becoming a reality.

Community life is changing and changing rapidly. With elderly clergy not being replaced and so few new ordinations, the situation is becoming very different, very quickly. We all need to act on our calling sooner rather than later, sharing our gifts and talents into the future. Lay people may begin to take on roles previously reserved for priests. They may lead liturgical celebrations in the absence of a priest, others will assist in sacramental preparation. We need to understand that lay people may minister to the sick, bring communion to the housebound. They may receive funerals at the church and officiate at the graveside.

Pastoral councils will become more involved in organising the various ministries in their areas and finance councils will assume greater responsibility. Educational and training programmes should be put in place. All these changes will take time to process mentally. I grew up attending a Catholic church with my parents. They were very different times. As I grew older, I met friends who were Protestant, Methodist, Presbyterian, and others. We had great discussions and as we did, most of us discovered we had so much in common.

Now as churches, we have even more in common as we are all struggling to keep the doors open. Is it because we are losing touch with the real world and its problems? There is little doubt we are becoming less effective at connecting with the next generation. The big question is, are we ready to reach out? Firstly, we need to begin with an honest self-assessment. That is what the Builders of Hope was all about.

Our church's approach is without doubt unappealing to our youth. I feel our young adults respect the core truths of Christianity, and in fact, I find them to be thoroughly moralistic. They want, above all else to live meaningful and fulfilling lives. The concept of reaching young people sounds great but how do we reach them?

We need to begin by changing our mindset. This book is built around looking at our past, understanding our strengths, and recognising our obstacles. Of course, most of us would like a magic pill to fix everything without making any effort. There is no such pill. The Pastoral Plan was not a magic pill, but it was a concrete way of moving forward.

There are things in the plan people will not agree with and there are things people will not want to hear. Builders of Hope was an integral part of my time as a pastoral worker. Every day I come across people who tell me their inspirational stories and I share them when I can. The more I travelled throughout the Diocese meeting people the more I realised we are not that different to each other. Neither are our communities as we go through very similar challenges.

We were all willing to learn but we have our different ways of doing it. Some will do it willingly and some will wait until a situation pushes them into it. We need to accept where our communities are at present. By being truthful we can embark on an exciting journey to develop and grow in a way that brings joy. Look at your community, the life within, and recognise what needs to change and what you hope to hold on to. After all, traditions are important. Keeping certain traditions alive for those coming after us will give them a sense of belonging.

This sense of belonging is very important to every member of the community. If we learn from the past, we can move on. If we keep doing the same thing, we will keep getting the same results. It is not good to stay stuck in the same pattern. It is all too easy to keep having the same conversations and to fill our schedules with all sorts of distractions, but we should stop and face up to things. Work out exactly what we want and work towards that.

We are the only ones who know what our community needs. Recognising what needs to change is perhaps the most difficult part of the process but once you have tackled that you will begin your way to becoming a vibrant, inclusive, and all-encompassing community. The only difference between achieving and not achieving is the conviction that you can.

Chapter Six

Pastoral: Experience and Vision

"To look at a thing is very different from seeing
it."
Oscar Wilde

The Role of the Pastoral Worker

The Pastoral Worker works in partnership with the priests and pastoral council of a parish or group of parishes promoting lifelong learning in tradition and Christian living. The pastoral worker shares in the work of supporting and encouraging a healthy relationship for all in the community. As a pastoral worker, I coordinated faith development initiatives taking into consideration the understanding of the Diocese of Killaloe and its mission.

I offered opportunities for various people to deepen their understanding of their faith and their community. I contributed to sacramental preparation programmes providing retreats for young people. I helped communities to find ways of enriching parish liturgical and sacramental celebrations. I encouraged and supported other lay people in living their faith within their community. I loved working with Parish Pastoral Councils, helping them in fulfilling their mission.

Being a pastoral worker, I assisted in the building of communities through trusting relationships. I tried to be available and fully 'present' to individuals and their needs as well as the community. Supporting and nurturing parish groups especially those engaged in the betterment of their communities was an essential part of my mission. Building links between home, school and parish was a number one priority.

Diocesan Pastoral Worker – My Experience

I returned to college as a mature student in September 2007. My children were all progressing in life and I was working unhappily in a job I disliked. Going to work every morning was a chore, I felt there must be more to life than getting up, going to work, coming home tired, eating, cleaning, going to bed only to wake up again the next day and start all over again. My daughter was preparing to go to college, and I was lamenting the fact that I did not the opportunity to go when I was her age.

It was then that I decided to shake up my life and begin to live the life I wanted. I applied to Mary Immaculate College as a mature student and was delighted to be accepted. This was an amazing time in my life. I planned to do English as I'd always wanted to write, as well as Psychology as I was really interested in helping others.

As part of my degree, I took four subjects for the first year. It was during this time I discovered Theology. I loved the subject and found myself veering towards it more and more. At the end of first year, I chose Theology over Psychology for no other reason than I felt drawn to it. I completed my honours degree and continued to postgraduate diploma and then my masters in adult and community education.

I loved college and I loved to study. It was after leaving college I found myself working with the Diocese of Killaloe. I saw the position advertised and thought 'it's not exactly what I am looking for, but it's bound to open some doors for me'. I was interviewed and to my delight, got the job. My first day was a revelation. I entered Bishop's House, a house I had always admired from afar.

I was invited in to have tea before beginning work at my office which was in Clarecastle. I was in the kitchen with some of the staff when the bishop came in. Who knew bishops drink tea?! I honestly did not know what to say or how to react. He introduced himself and very soon put me at ease.

Here I was, a mother of three adult children, a recent college graduate, confident in all areas of my life but I reverted to my childhood in the presence of the hierarchy. I realised on reflection that everything I had fought for as a woman I still allowed my patriarchal conditioning to raise its ugly head.

I settled into my new position getting to know the bishop, the clergy and the diocesan staff and volunteers. I found them to be people of immense faith who only wanted the best for their community. I worked for the Diocese for over five years. I worked in partnership with the priests, pastoral councils, cluster areas and the diocese as they promoted the mission of the Church at a local level.

As Pastoral Worker, I was involved in encouraging parishioner participation, in new initiatives through the implementation of the pastoral plan. Other parts of the role involved building community and enhancing the authenticity of the parish. Building relationships throughout the diocese was an important and enjoyable part of my responsibilities.

It was all very new to me having spent all my working life in administration. I loved working for the diocese. Initially, I met with all the clergy and all the pastoral councils. Not everyone was happy with my message which was one of change and collaboration. I found the clergy were aware of the challenging situation in which they found themselves.

The laity on the other hand seemed to think that a priest would be found somewhere if one was needed. This of course is no longer the case. Priests are overworked within their own parish, but they are now responsible for more than one parish. My message may not have been welcomed but thankfully I was made to feel welcome.

I was encouraged to put new ideas forward, to try new initiatives and be seen as part of the diocese. It was good for the community to see a lay person and a woman in a leadership role. I was confident and happy in this role. I was passionate about the work I was doing. In the beginning, people did not understand my role. Maybe they felt I was a spy for the diocese. This could not be further from the truth. I was there to support them as volunteers around their local community.

During the listening process two years beforehand, there was constant mention of people not knowing their role within the community. I began by providing workshops for pastoral councils to discuss their role. I was blown away by the attendance at each workshop. I was 'Marie', the lady from the diocese, and I was fitting in. People were so welcoming. It was heartening to see that at times of change and challenge in our Church people still had hope.

These people are committed to making their Church and their faith community the best they can be. We live in a modern society that often compels us to live in completely conflicting ways, but we are doing our best to work together in our community. To make them better places. Places where our children will grow and love. For many years I had been involved in parish work, Minister of the Word, Minister of the Eucharist and choir.

I was involved in the areas of Spirituality, involving prayer facilitation and adult faith formation. As a young woman, my life revolved around playing the organ (badly) at church services.

When the Diocese of Killaloe introduced the role of Diocesan Pastoral Worker, I saw it as an opportunity to bring together my work-life skills and my existing activities in the church to help in the development of the church in the diocese. This role is in answer to Vatican II to encourage and utilise the gifts and talents of the laity.

My role as a Diocesan Pastoral Worker challenged me every day. It challenged me in my faith, and in how I support other people in theirs. I make every effort to do this by example. I am open honest and express my concern and compassion for my community openly. Most community leaders I know don't want to keep their churches small, they care about growing and progressing. They want to extend the hand of welcome and reach out to more people. They want to see their goals achieved and their mission fully realized. They look forward to the day when they can reach as many people as they can within their community. Anyone involved in Church will know this is not easy.

The Diocese of Killaloe is no different from any other in the country in that they see their attendance at Church dwindling in recent years. One priest said his 'was a grey congregation' in that all his participants in Church were older members of the community. I have to say in my journeys throughout the Diocese while speaking at Masses, I was pleasantly surprised at the number of people in the pews. Where I saw the most energy was where the community leaders took a special interest in their community and where lay participation was fostered and encouraged.

In the Churches where pray-and-play was active and young people were encouraged to take part, there was a great vitality in the service. A liveliness of the whole community celebrating together.

If we figure out how to tackle the issue of pastoral work and pastoral care in the community, we will grow. It is left to the priest because it is seen as his job, but the laity can do so much more. When the priest must visit every sick person, do every funeral, perform at every wedding, make regular home visits all the while attending every meeting, preparing for the sacraments, leading community groups, attending diocesan meetings they soon become like hamsters on a training wheel. Going around and around doing their best but eventually becoming burnt out.

It is ironic if the priest is a good pastoral care person, the members of his community will love and depend on him so much that the pastoral care expectations may become crushing. The priest tries to keep up but sometimes they cannot and end up disappointing people.

As communities, it would be great if we could look to the pastoral care we can provide. There were many discussions around this topic when I visited Pastoral Councils. They agreed laity are more than capable of performing many pastoral care duties. We could, for instance, visit the sick. We all know that especially for the older generation they like to see their priest, but they would be delighted with any visit concerned with their welfare.

Many of the priests I know like to please people by their nature. They want to be caring in their community and they hate to disappoint. But because there are fewer priests now their reach needs to extend even further.

In the past, the parishioners relied on their priests for their care needs as well as their spiritual needs. This is a mindset that needs to change. Most do not want this to change. They saw the need for change and most pastoral councils were willing to take on more of the pastoral needs of the community but there was fear. This was a fear that the community would not accept them as caregivers. Fear that they would not be good enough to give that care. We do not need to be ordained to care for our community. We do not need a PhD. We need common sense, life experience and a caring nature. For specific duties within the community or Church, training can be provided.

A priest once told me 'If we have people with the passion for community and Church, we can provide them with the knowledge'. This is so true. We all find our identity and character within our immediate environment, and we often look to our community for fulfilment. Maybe the more we care for that community the more we will improve our self-worth. It could also be said that our priest's look to their parishioners to provide them with a sense of self-worth and fulfilment. Most of us like to be needed and our priest is no different. I found that many parishes defined the success of their priest on how available they are. They also focused on how likeable and friendly they were, rather than how efficient or organized they tended to be.

Likability seems to be a benchmark for effective Christian leadership in our culture. I am not sure our priests would see it in this way. Of course, they like to be liked but it was my experience that a priest sees the goal of Christian leadership is to lead but not always necessary to be liked. Sometimes it is more essential to do what is best for all rather than what people want.

While attending gatherings it was my understanding that the parishioners still expected that their priest would be available for every celebration, every crisis, and every community predicament. This is a mindset we need to break. We need to begin the shift of pastoral care to the community with all of us together co-responsible.

It is much healthier than what happened in the past. We need the courage to take that leap. Some people only want their priest and that is fine while we have a priest, but the time might come when there is no priest available. Who then will bury our dead? We should prepare now. We need to instil in people that they can care for each other. We cannot do it alone. We need leaders but they can be lay leaders.

I feel this message is seeping through. The transition is starting. I believe that ninety per cent of pastoral care is having someone to listen to and someone to care, it does not always have to be the priest. Of course, there are times and situations where only our priest will do but we need to begin to take the life experience and training of our parishioners into account. Most communities will have professional counsellors, carers, teachers, medics who would be happy to help in their community. We should make use of these abilities. Every person in the community has something to offer.

In Killaloe, the discussion is ongoing. We need to prepare for the future and that does not mean giving up on what we had but embracing and sharing new ways. We can grow again if we all take part in our pastoral care. In my mind, it is simply unfeasible for a community to flourish under one person's direct care and leadership. We all need to lead in sharing our gifts and talents.

Perhaps we should get over the apprehension and worry of disappointing people. We need to be courageous and do what we believe is best and what will nourish our community into the future. Group caring and outreach will touch more people. Pastoral care can refer to spiritual guidance, counselling, and visitation. Its core concept is to care.

The word pastor comes from the Latin word for shepherd. A pastor is to be a shepherd or caretaker. Shepherds take care of their flock, their community. We all have the capabilities to be shepherds. Many people have a misunderstanding of what exactly pastoral care is. Pastoral care in the community is extremely valuable. Caring for a person who is struggling or under pressure with stress. Being present with someone in a time of crisis is beneficial both to the receiver and the giver.

Ministering through your personal touch is one of the most valuable gifts you can share with your community. While meeting Pastoral Councils I got the feeling that pastoral care today needs re-thinking. As Church, we have grown into a limited experience of pastoral care. We see pastoral care as comforting the sick or bereaved and of course, it is, but it is much, more.

The truth is we all need pastoral care. We all need nurturing. Our inherited model of pastoral care needs to be challenged. We need a more holistic approach to the pastoral care of our whole community. A more inclusive approach. It can be as simple as reaching out to a neighbour or friend with a coffee.

In my view, there are several clear goals for pastoral development. We need to communicate. Anyone who knows me knows how I believe there is no substitute for communication. We can never over-communicate. People must know what is happening.

We also need to establish what we mean by pastoral care so we can all grow as caring, compassionate communities. Pastoral care is essentially about supporting one another into the fullness of life within our communities. Pastoral care is for all. It is also about the whole of life, not just about our participation in the life of our Church.

Pastoral care is not just about relief in painful or sorrowful situations. Paul spells out that all of us should come together to mature and grow in Christ. It is not about each of us doing it individually but about finding full maturity in a Faith Community. Pastoral care is mutual care with each of us caring for the other.

Re-imagining Pastoral Care in the community is in the interest of inclusivity into the future. It is all about the care of people and their relationships. Each community will need to work out what suits its situation best. Each community is unique. Nonetheless helping one another to grow in love and fulfilment is widespread. My experience during my time as a pastoral worker was that people really did want to help each other. Communities always came together in times of crisis.

Growing pastoral care was an issue that came up regularly at gatherings. People felt there were several things they could do at a local level to improve their community. It was felt that drawing together a group of people with a particular focus could be a way forward. One area for instance felt there was a growing need for a bereavement group in their area. Growing a group of people to serve the whole community should be a long-term goal. It is not something that can happen overnight. This group were determined to find like-minded people who could provide a much-needed service for their community.

They began the process of gathering people with a genuine interest in supporting the bereaved. It was open to everyone in the community. For three months, twenty-one people gathered with the same goal in mind. It has been my experience that connecting with others in times of need is invaluable.

When we lose someone we love, we often feel the need to connect with others who understand what we are going through. Support groups can give us a safe place to interact with others. A place where we can discuss our feelings without fear of being judged. This is what this community group wanted to do. They wanted to provide a safe space. They attended an information night and continued by attending six nights of training.

For me, this group was one of the nicest bunch of people I have ever met. They had some wonderful unintrusive ideas of how they could bring their community together in times of grief. This community identified a need, understood that they could provide pastoral care and sought training.

They offered their skills, their prior lived experience, as well as their training to their community where everyone can benefit. A true way of delivering holistic pastoral care to the community.

As a Pastoral Worker listening is the starting point and a vital element in the gathering of information. It is a form of 'pastoral market research' which is necessary to gaining and obtaining insights into the hopes and struggles of community life. In looking towards pastoral development, we all need to be comfortable with each other. Building relationships with each other is key. Moving away from a hierarchical way of functioning would be in the interest of all.

Giving and receiving mutual support is what it is all about. People have confidence in the integrity of others. I found that when matched by real listening there is learning for the whole community. The more indication that genuine listening has taken place, the more likely it is that building hope will be accepted.

Pastoral care is based on empathy not on expertise. Sharing a common humanity with all in the community can only further pastoral care. Many feel that our culture of individualism and independence is more important than our relationship with our community. We see how we live out our lives as our own business. Most people yearn for the comradery of youth. The value of community, the value of belonging cannot be underestimated.

A conscious policy of working across the community to gather opinions allows a relationship of trust to develop. People are very open when they are listened to. When they feel their opinions and ideas lead to action, they are happy to get involved in the process.

It is when people feel they are not being heard that stagnation sets in. Supporting each other in our communities leads to a growing of pastoral relationships and the holistic approach of mutual understanding. The views of the people within the community need to be taken seriously.

It is all those who live in the community regardless of age, status, gender, or bias who will shape the community of the future. In setting up new initiatives and holding relevant events there is a hope and expectation that pastoral care will be enabled.

Those involved in leadership and guidance may need to re-work certain facets considered to be negative. Communication of the vision going forward is vital. In communicating the insights gained from the community and the vision for the future everyone will have an input, and everyone will know what to expect. Co-operation is key.

People are more reluctant to become involved if they do not feel capable. They are afraid they are not good enough and they are afraid of being ridiculed within their own community. A lot can be done to provide training for those participating in their community. In receiving training, people will become more confident. Providing a workshop where members of the community can explore the variety of skills and life experiences available, may open the minds and hearts of many helping them understand exactly what they have to offer. People have a lot more to offer than they realise.

One of the most frequently voiced concerns I heard in my journey as a Pastoral Worker was that of the lack of communication, not least with the leaders but across all spectrums. Addressing this issue is essential. If good communication is delivered, people will respect the process.

The number of priests in Ireland is decreasing. Our priests are getting older, and yet there seems to be more work than ever to be done. Throughout the years many priests gave themselves to a faithful ministry serving their communities in an exemplary way while others eroded trust by their blatant misuse of authority.

The time has come when we need to look to the future. Lay Pastoral Workers, bring a spirit of renewal to our communities. Many Pastoral Councils make this clear.

We are not a substitute for priests, but we are capable of providing pastoral care and other ministries in the community.

The ongoing participation of lay people in parish and community life should be encouraged. The priest has a unique mission. The priesthood is a calling. It is not simply a job or a function to be carried out on occasion. It is not for me to explain priesthood because I cannot. I believe priesthood to be a mission. A mission in knowing Jesus and being like him in every aspect of their life. A priest once told me that his way of life comes especially from prayer, and on a continuous reflection of scripture.

I believe we too have a calling. A calling to live our own authentic life. There is an increasing commitment of lay people to take up theology and pastoral development courses. These gifts and talents should be utilized.

By becoming co-responsible with our priests, we can re-structure our communities. Paul tells us that we should 'Welcome each other... without grumbling. Each one of you has received a special grace, so like good stewards responsible for all these different graces of God, put yourselves at the service of others'.

In my experience as a pastoral worker, I found people to be so kind and genuinely interested in the survival of their communities. There was a lot of good energy, but it is fair to say there was also a lot of jealousy. Some were reluctant to entertain any new ideas in fear of losing power.

They saw it as a power struggle and put obstacles in the way of moving forward. There were letters written questioning the new methods and indeed the qualifications of those providing a new way forward.

Thankfully, I had all the qualifications needed and I was very happy to share ideas, provide training, and sit with the people who felt they were being left out or over-shadowed. These people are integral to our way forward. After all, most had experience and skills essential to moving forward. We are all in this together.

I have no doubt the bigger picture for the future will be very different. We can draw from the lessons of our past even if they have changed radically. Now more than ever there is a search for meaning and wellbeing.

We had meaning and purpose in our past through parental influence. Family life was strong, and we had visible role models. We had more sharing between generations and across communities. We were more concerned about who we were rather than what we did and what we had. Back then we had very little compared to now.

Growing up in Broadford I thought things would never change and the village was my world. But things did change. I was one of the lucky ones securing a job in the civil service and moving to Dublin. Even though I never settled there, I learned a lot from the experience. I travelled extensively, had a family, and went on to find purpose in education.

Returning to education as a mature student was one of the best experiences of my life and allowed me to work with the diocese of Killaloe. My time as a pastoral worker was a real learning curve for me. I had a degree in theology and met many other lay people with theology degrees and some with masters. But knowing is one thing, watching people live religion is a whole other dimension. It is so important that we do not ignore or lose touch with the lived experience of all those in our community.

Very often people who have experienced struggle are the best people to understand the plight of others. Many draw their sense of worth from their family and community. I gained a huge sense of worth from working as a pastoral worker. It was a vivid, fulfilling experience for me.

Yes, there were a lot of critics of what we were hoping to achieve but there were so many more who wanted to see change, even embrace it. I was inspired and amazed by the people I met. We all knew things had gone wrong and we were working towards a communal goal. We need to start doing something about it.

Each group I met allowed me to connect with people. Their support helped me connect in a meaningful way. Meeting with different groups of people with a similar goal helped me honour who I was and what I wanted in life. Supporting each other helped us to create deeper, more meaningful relationships. This in turn helped us fuel our minds and our spirits.

Building a meaningful community is a deliberate process in bringing people together to support each other. The truth is it takes commitment and action to support people in our community and the people I met with had that commitment. We need to harness that.

Most people are open, willing, and very interested in making their community the best it can be. Building supportive communities happens a step at a time. The possibility for supportive caring communities exists all around us, we simply need to open our eyes, open our mouths, open our ears and most importantly, open our hearts.

My experience of being a Pastoral worker was amazing. It was an experience of great personal growth.

I can only hope that in the process I was of inspiration to those I met and to those involved in pastoral ministry as well as to parish pastoral councils. I hope I offered opportunities for them to see a way forward for their communities.

Pastoral Worker – The vision

When I began with the Diocese of Killaloe, I was not fully aware of what the future of the community would look like. There were challenges ahead. There was a thirst for something different. Something new. The old way of viewing the parish or community was getting tired in people's eyes. However, some would never want to change. But if we want to evolve, we need to change.

I tried to visualise the kind of community I would like to live in and be involved with. My vision is simply mine and no one else's. The community I would love to be a part of is one of care and compassion. Not one where everyone knows and does everything perfectly but one where everyone is willing to learn and willing to try.

I would like us to see ourselves as deeper thinkers and to look at ourselves as being spiritual. There is a new mood taking hold. There may be a sense of complacency but there is also a sense of hope.

The vision going forward is a community that reaches out. We should look back and learn from our strong heritage, our strong traditions, our strong rituals but we must not go on as before. A priest once told me 'why change, this will see me out'. He gave of himself all his life and he was tired. He no longer wanted challenges or change.

Why not let him live out his servitude but his community could be exploring new ways of engaging with people.

Creativity is the way forward. Finding new ways of 'being' in our communities. Keeping our core alive but exploring new possibilities brings a sense of hope. Listening to the people in the community and appreciating what they have to say will bring a new spiritual depth. Yes, keep our roots and our beliefs but engage in a deeper more profound way of being 'community'. Be appreciative of what everyone has to say and what everyone believes. Goodness and compassion can be active in all kinds of ways to people of all kinds of beliefs.

Where a community allows itself to be open and listen to people it will be enriched. I have seen this happen time and time again. There are so many ways in which people are living their spiritual lives. Many of them outside of the church. Surely a community should be inclusive of all.

When we learn from others, we become deeper and stronger in our faith and become more aware of who we are. A community that connects with all. A community that becomes spiritually rich. If we are considerate of people and where they are, we will take root and grow. Compassion and care bring relevant to people's lives.

We all need compassion, and it is best when it comes from our own communities. Finding new ways of expressing ourselves is a way to the future. Re-connecting with people how and when they need it will see a richer community emerge.

When I look to the future and my vision for my community I look to Broadford and other communities like it. It is not about self-preservation or expansion but about taking what we know from our past, adding to it and creating a real sense of belonging for everyone. Focus not on who or what people are but on how we can connect with them and care for them. Compassion should be our driver.

I love parables and I believe they provide us with very good lessons on how to treat each other. My favourite would have to be the 'Good Samaritan'. We can learn a lot from this: 'Love the Lord your God with all your heart and with all your soul and with all your strength and with all your mind Love your neighbour as yourself'. (Luke 10:25-37). If we love our neighbour as ourselves, we will have the best community possible.

Another vision I have is where everyone contributes to their community. We are all working towards the same goal where we share a future vision. We are all community. Wouldn't it be great if our community was a sanctuary where we know we are all cared for? Where we can take shelter and find love. Where we can find purpose and meaning.

When we welcome and connect with others in our community, we will find all the support we need. When we gather in compassion we will be companions on this wonderful journey of life. Jesus practised table fellowship. This is a wonderful way of being together sharing meals with others. Breaking bread with others helps us all connect.

Our vision for the future is a participative community, a home, a place of welcome and inclusion. A compassionate community is one where people grow together in love. Where people are fully 'present' not self-absorbed or preoccupied.

Experiencing inclusion and connection leads us to a feeling of belonging. How do we achieve this? We can make it as difficult or as simple as we like. I like to think simple is the way to go.

Begin by welcoming people and letting them feel connected.

We can do that by listening and accepting where they are right now. Once people feel respected and accepted, they will feel welcome and in turn, will contribute. Giving people the opportunity to contribute without judgement is difficult for some but it is important. We all need a generous spirit of compassion towards others. This will bring about hope for the future. Growing in compassion together will nourish and enrich our community.

Caring and ministering to each other is what community is all about. We are very good at community in Ireland. We are rooted in care and compassion. Our communities are mostly ministering communities.

Our Irish language is unique to us, and the words care, and ministry comes together in the word 'Aire'. We certainly care in Ireland, and we are at our best when we are ministering care to others. There is so much care in our homes from the little child who hurts their knee and mum, or dad kisses it better, to the care of our older family members. Often people themselves do not recognise the care they are ministering.

Our family is our first place of belonging and in most families, there is an abundance of love and care for each other. Our family is our first community where we live out love and belonging and care for others. Our first place of ministering. I was very lucky to grow up in a loving caring family. Don't get me wrong, we were not perfect, and we didn't always like each other but we always loved each other.

Whether we are coming from a faith perspective or a humanitarian perspective all our care in the community creates a space of belonging.

A community where all people live together in a caring supportive existence is a community where everyone wants to live.

From a young age, I wanted to be a mother. It really was my only goal in life. I tried to be the best mother I could be, but I know I had weaknesses. A few years ago, I was at a talk and the gentleman talking was discussing our mission in life. 'We all have a mission' he said. It was that evening I discovered my mission was 'to be a mother'. My children are all grown up now but my mission as a mother continues. However, it is not my only mission. I am happiest when I am caring, and I care for my family, friends, and my community.

The vision I see as a Pastoral Worker is one of connection between the love we share in our families and the love we share in communities.

Our communities in the past were predominately Catholic. Although Catholicism is still the backbone of our Irish communities most people do not practice it. Looking to the future maybe we should look to bringing together a broad range of people and groups where care rather than religion is the common denominator.

Our communities are deepened by encouraging everyone to contribute. Building an inclusive community connects life, love, and spirituality. It unites everyone. An inclusive, caring community is the vision for the future. A community with a common focus. One where all will live in harmony. Is this possible? I believe it is.

To find it we should move beyond the walls of the church. Move beyond the institution. Move beyond hierarchy. The vision would be to offer a friendly, caring, supportive face to the community. Look to ways of offering support.

One such community who does this is the community of Kilbane in Co. Clare. Their church was closed due to lack of priests. I believe when the church closes, the people will take over. After all the people are the Church.

The people of Kilbane no longer have a priest presiding over their Church but it is not lying idle. As a community they are bringing new life to their Church building by opening it up to the community.

They continue in a religious vein, by honouring the saints, in producing an information wall venerating the saint of the day. They offer arts and crafts, a book exchange and they hope couples will choose to get married there. This is survival.

St Mary's Church Kilbane being brought back to life
Photo Niamh Quinn

I would like to mention one other parish that looked to ways of supporting their community. They wanted to provide support to the bereaved in their community. They were a group of concerned people in West Clare in the areas of Mullagh and Kilmurry-Ibrickane. They came together as a focus group in Mullagh and committed to providing support to the bereaved in the community. They had a vision and they made it happen.

This is where I met Peggy, the ultimate community woman. Peggy was always on hand to help out, she even offered me accommodation on a stormy night so I didn't have to drive the long road home. I didn't know then, but, Peggy was Peggy Morrissey, Marty's mum. She lived her life for her faith and for her community.

Tabhair-Aire – The vision

Three years ago, I provided a workshop in Spanish Point for the people of the Criocha Callan pastoral area. This workshop explored the needs of the surrounding area and how this focus group could reach out. There was a robust discussion that night and many ideas were delved into. It came to the fore that they would like to explore the idea of providing a bereavement group. They felt it would benefit the area. I was approached to deliver the training and I was delighted to oblige.

On the first night of training, I drove over the mountain into Mullagh, to the community hall, not knowing who or what to expect. We needed at least ten people to make the training worthwhile. I was overwhelmed to find so many waiting for me. They were some of the nicest, most caring people I have ever met.

We began our training every Monday evening for eight weeks. Everyone gave their all to the project. Each person committed to becoming more conscious of their community and its needs. They were a caring group who grew in awareness of their wider community.

Jesus told us to care for one another as he did, and this is what the 'Tabhair Aire' group was all about. After all the clue was in the name 'Tabhair Aire', 'Take Care'. This group was not just a group at prayer they were a group at care. They gave their skills, talents, and training to be there for others in their community in their time of need.

Working with them I invited them to think of what they were about. They felt they wanted to be at the heart of their community, to be there if people needed them. They also knew the importance of standing back. This community made me feel like I belonged. I cherished their commitment and their sense of community. They were adept at inviting people into an experience of belonging and welcome. This I believe is the vision for the future. It demonstrates that all communities can aspire to be the best that they can be.

Week after week I saw them getting stronger and more confident in themselves and their ability. After all, they were not going to be professionals in the field of grief, but they were together in their commonality of caring.

Above all, they were a welcoming group. They describe themselves as a locally-based, voluntary bereavement support group in their community in West Clare, where they aim to support those bereaved in their community. They have a voluntary helpline to offer support and guidance.

Their mission statement is 'We aspire to take care of our bereaved community to the best of our ability.' How can any community do more?

They inspired me. They showed me there are people out there with skills and talents but above all with warm, caring hearts. I left with a graduation ceremony where every member received certification. It was a night of joy.

They had the training. They had the will to reach out. The rest was now up to them.

I was invited back on the night they launched their booklet and themselves into the community. It was an uplifting and moving night.

Two speakers told of their own experiences, and they were so eloquent, understanding and open, I knew this group would make a difference in their community. After all who can provide support better than those with lived experience. This was only one group I met in my travels throughout the Diocese of Killaloe. They had a vision, acted on it, and brought it to the community.

All the groups I met were enthusiastic about exploring new visions and indeed many of them brought their ideas to fruition. Some of the possibilities considered were family Masses, child-friendly Masses, greeters at the doors, welcome banners in different languages, tea after Mass, faith friends, funeral teams, training for readers, eucharist ministers, visitation teams. Focus groups were formed, they would look at how they could bring something meaningful to their community.

The Church in the past was clerical with little or no input from lay people. The church is now becoming more participative where everyone's input is considered important.

Mullagh Parish Church (Photo Marie O'Connell)

Is it too late to make a difference?

The Killaloe Diocese continues building hope and optimism. Central to this is one very significant progression, which they call the New Ministries where twenty-four lay people graduated with a qualification in Pastoral Care and Catechetics. This can only be a good thing. It is very common to feel we cannot make a difference but remember, many have been in this position before, and they succeeded. The important thing is not to fear trying.

Many communities stay stuck in the familiar. It is good to leave our comfort zones and bring something new to the table, to examine our agenda. Many of us are guilty of letting our ego get in the way as I know I have many times. Becoming better listeners is very important. Sitting back and listening to others can be a very enlightening and freeing experience. If someone in the community is very opinionated and is always the first to comment it can be very difficult for others to show their interest.

Perhaps we could all be open-minded and flexible in our behaviour.

It is never too late to make a difference in the community, but we all need to be open to it. Navigating together will make us stronger.

A lovely woman I know who wrote poetry always wanted to publish a book. She felt she was too old, and it was too late. We persuaded her it was never too late so in her ninetieth year she published her book of poetry...proving that it is never too late.

As communities, we should begin to walk the walk as soon as possible. Talking the talk is important, but if that is all we do, people lose interest, and our hopes and dreams remain in our heads.

We should try to be innovative and turn those hopes and dreams into reality. Easy? No. It is not easy and that is why we give up. We need commitment, perseverance, and willpower. Our goals may seem unobtainable at first, but by breaking them down into action steps, keeping our vision, we can turn them into reality. I always wanted to be a teacher but could not go to college. I never let my goal go and became a teacher as a mature student. That may sound simplistic, but it was all about building up my confidence and belief in myself.

We have several chapters in our lives and once we are happy and healthy, we are already winning. In transferring our confidence, our spirit, and our happiness to our communities, we can really make a difference. One person can make a difference. Recently, in my local community, a man fed up with the litter situation put a post on Facebook, stating he would be picking it up at nine o'clock on Saturday morning if anyone wanted to join him. Twenty people turned up. A simple gesture that built to this group coming together on several local projects. Recognising the need in the community is the starting point.

It is always a good idea to brainstorm, look at the bigger picture, the result you want, and work from there. Making mistakes along the way is inevitable. We all have a fear of failing but it is best to put this fear behind us. Focus on what we are good at, look at the skills available and go for it. Look to other communities, researching what you want. Believe in yourselves as a community and listen to all the voices.
Involve as many people as possible. People really care about their community and will help if possible.

Map out where we need to go and take it one step at a time. For instance, some communities like to set up new groups like bereavement groups, memorial committees, care groups, youth teams, whatever it is, and it is always good to start with some brainstorming.

Inclusivity in community endeavours is very important. It is also good to consider training. Getting started, achieving small victories, and creating action steps is key. It comes down to the needs and wants of the community in which we are living. Most communities have historical traditions they want to preserve. The heart and soul are the same today as they were in our youth and our parent's youth. I am a firm believer we can find the passion we need. We do not need to believe in God or be a member of any religion to get in touch with our spiritual essence.

Although no longer a pastoral worker with the Diocese of Killaloe, I am happy to move on to new things. One thing I learned is the continued need to grow spiritually. Meditation for me is about finding your inner spirit, a sanctuary of calmness and depth.

In meditation, we can enhance our sense of self, which allows us to develop spiritually. Meditation is no longer for the cloistered communities but is available to everyone.

It is not easy to begin with, but practice makes perfect. There are many schools of meditation and many different styles but they all hinge on our personal experience. Offering a meditative or reflective space in the community would benefit all. Meditation brings me feelings of peace, stillness, and grace. It helps me to think clearly and deeply. I find my creativity deepens and grows.
I am now, after a lifetime of different experiences, living my best life. I accredit this to experience, meditation, and my supportive community.

While working with the Diocese of Killaloe, I was introduced to spiritual guidance. It explores the spiritual aspects of our being and helps us explore our sense of meaning and purpose. It can help us develop a deeper relationship with ourselves and it helps us renew our sense of the sacred with our own deep 'self'. Spiritual guidance has occurred historically in almost every cultural and spiritual tradition.

As Celtic people, we have a very spiritual tradition, which awakens us to the fullness and mystery of life. Once we become spiritually aware we become complete, we are 'home.' This is the best feeling of all. From the earliest times, we here in Ireland felt the need to answer the call of the hallowed ground. For me, there is no better place than to be in tune with nature. Our ancestors felt themselves to be in contact with the spirits that lay beyond this world of ours.

Our Celtic roots communicated our connection with the spirit in sacred carvings and dance and ritual.

The meeting of Celtic spirituality and Christianity in Ireland put forward a treasure of wisdom regarding the presence of something bigger. It encompassed a message of love and compassion. This is all we need. We should honour and welcome all that is good and helpful in our traditions. We recognize that people walk many different paths towards the Mystery, which calls them.

We in Ireland are privileged to have a wealth of stories, history, folklore and legends about the women and men who walked before us. Many people identify themselves as spiritual but not religious. An instinct toward spirituality seems to be deep-rooted in us humans.

We love to ask big questions. I know I ask the question daily. I love finding new ways of expressing myself and finding inner peace. It has taken me years of evolving through pain and happiness, but I feel I have arrived with an inner self I like. I have reinvented myself several times, all to be comfortable in my own skin.

I know more than anyone that reinvention is not an overnight job. It takes courage, perseverance, and hard work but we all need to reinvent from time to time. Our communities are no different. Let us take the steps we need to achieve our goals both personally and in our communities. As we do, we will grow in confidence.

As a teacher, tutor, pastoral worker, and life coach I believe we can evolve to develop new ways of living. Communities are no different. We have been evolving in Ireland for centuries and we will certainly continue to do so as our young people begin to have their voices heard.

We must be open to new opportunities. In the middle of chaos, opportunities may be missed, therefore, it is important to stay aware.

The change starts with us. It is all about the small but conscious decisions we make every day. If we become aware of how we speak to ourselves and begin to change our mindset, we will be the change we want. Having the belief in our communities will help us achieve our goals.

Making any sort of change in the beginning can be very overwhelming. Picture your end goal and find the courage to start now. Sometimes we need to go with the flow of life, but the important thing is to keep going with our action steps.
Use all the talent available to you and let go of any ego-based decisions. Commit to your goal and embrace it.

I believe we learned from our Covid experience. During all the uncertainty and challenges faced, this period helped many evaluate their lives and focus on what is truly important. It served as a reminder of how precious life is and how to appreciate the little things. We found balance. None of us knew when normality would resume, but we walked in our lovely surroundings taking the time to say hello across the road. We needed human contact. We lived with uncertainty the best way we knew how. We had to adapt.

This pandemic was disastrous to our world but it has been a testament to how robust and resilient we are. It also gave us time to rest and recharge. Certainly, we are far more aware of the beauty of our great outdoors. Wherever I went, I saw people walking, hiking, and biking; families playing and being together. Our communities moved outside, and we all seem healthier and happier for it. We realised the essentials are all we need. As we begin to kick-start our communities, it will be good to remember what Covid meant to us.

I live in my new community of Ballina/Killaloe. I love it here. It enjoys many of the traditions I grew up with.

Owing its origin to a sixth-century monastic settlement founded by Saint Molua in the tenth century, Killaloe was also the base for Brian Boru. He had his palace on the high ground where the current Catholic church now stands.

Killaloe was effectively the capital of Ireland between 1002 and 1014 while Brian was high king. Living in the area, I often visit his fort. It is a place of peace and tranquillity, a community of the past. Another place of merit and a building that holds a special space in my heart is St Flannan's Cathedral (Church of Ireland) built between 1185 and 1225.

The space within these walls saved my sanity. This ancient building freed me to be imperfect, make mistakes, continue to grow, and find purpose. I am very proud and happy to live here now, although my heart lies in Broadford, more and more of it is resting in Ballina/Killaloe.

I feel this community came together in the crisis. It made a difference. The community rallied around, and new community leaders were born. We can only hope that this collective action will continue and will be the key to creating a better future for all of us.

There have been many changes in Ireland in the past one hundred years. It was a country of extremes where many dwellings were large homes with ten or more rooms, and many were one-room tenements. This has changed dramatically. Most marriages were Catholic, but this has dropped now to under sixty per cent. Life expectancy has increased strongly in the past one hundred years, with the greatest increases for younger age groups.

There were nearly 10,000 cars in Ireland in 1921, with cars registered in every county while by 2021 there were 2.3 million private cars.

There have been many changes in Irish society, but our communities still lie at the heart of community life, and we can all make a difference. Our community is our life.

Who will bury our dead?

Our community may be our light but who in the community will bury our dead? We have established that all religious communities are in trouble and the Catholic Church in Ireland is in crisis. With many communities now functioning without a priest who will lead our traditional services? Even if we never go inside a Church when a loved one dies, we still look to the Church in our grief. When will we start planning for the dead of the future? Have you considered if a loved one dies and there is no longer a priest in your community, who will you turn to? Would you consider a spiritual director from another denomination? We need to debate these questions. We can bury our heads in the sand but the truth is in five years' time we will have considerably less priests.

At the beginning of each year churches in Ireland, pray for unity, but what do they mean by this? If we really mean we pray for unity why do we not unite? As all Christian religions are under threat, why not unite with one another and build a different future? Perhaps we could focus on the bonds between the priesthood of all believers. After all, every Christian is called to recognise the gifts and talents of others.

Every Christian is equipped to walk together and live in spiritual union with one another. It would be wonderful to deepen a collaboration of all the Christian Churches.

Together we would be stronger. This may seem Utopian, but it is not impractical. It would mean individual denominations co-existing and co-operating as much as possible, but this is all down to respect.

Is that respect there? I believe it can be. The way forward is to look at what is happening within the churches themselves and all churches are struggling. They would be stronger together than apart. If there is no priest to bury our dead maybe a vicar could, or maybe a monk could or maybe lay people trained in the community could.

Many worry that unity would mean the loss of independence. It is true to say that Churches value denominational identity in the same manner as a nation's value national identity. We manage to unite as countries so why not as Churches.

The vision may be difficult to define but we need to start the conversation. We need solutions going forward, why not go forward together? There are encouraging signs of a broader vision for an ecumenical movement, which moves beyond structures. This is what we need. The vision voiced is that the goal cannot be limited to church unity but involves the unity of all humankind. After all, mission in the New Testament includes issues of justice and peace and the integrity of creation.

This would seem the direction in which the ecumenical effort has been drawn in the last decade. What I put forward here is very simplistic. I know to look at an ecumenical future would require much conversation and commitment, but it would be worth it.

As with all movements, the future of the Ecumenical movement will certainly see a shift towards spirituality. Like all other movements, they will need lay participation. In essence, we need lay leadership in our communities.

On balance, we do not need a degree in theology nor to be of a certain religion, to celebrate our loved ones lives respectfully. Sometimes relevant life experience is more appropriate than a PhD. However, training could be provided.

In the past, we saw other Churches as competitors or the enemy. I hope that this is no longer the case. When I sit in St Flannan's Cathedral, I think of my grandparents, and how they would feel about me sitting inside the door of a non-Catholic Church. I am sure they would frown. Thankfully, we are now able to look past this.

Pope Benedict said that ecumenism, rooted in truth and love, is not some luxury. It is at the core of the essential mission of the church. There are, of course, core questions dividing Christians, but can we not strive for unity in diversity with diverse gifts.

It would be wonderful if we could all become grounded together, supporting each other in our yearning for peace and understanding. If we listen carefully to all the voices, our doctrinal dialogue would be simplified. Understanding life and caring for our community is significant. Working together for a brighter future.

As members of the communities we serve, we want our neighbours to feel safe and well. Together, we can pursue inventive solutions to improve our collective experience. We can address the key challenges of today's world.

With our society moving at a faster pace, we have become increasingly detached from each other. It is harder and harder to feel a sense of community.

For generations, our community served an important role by acting as a support system. This support resurfaced during this pandemic.

Nobody understands a community better than those who live there.

A strong community benefits individuals, the community itself, and the greater society. Feeling a sense of belonging leads to happier and healthier lives. Strong communities create a more stable and supportive society. This is what we all want.

During Covid, we once more put our heart back into the community, and we benefited. Let us hope we can look to the future now and consider those difficult questions. Who will bury our dead? In putting the heart back in our community and keeping it ticking we can and will survive.

Throughout this book, I shared my story and my experience so you will know I have walked the walk. I am aware of how some communities struggle and others soar. Throughout the experience, I have been a student as I continuously evolve and develop. Seeing both sides of a situation permit me to bring a flexible approach.

I hope we can take a more flexible approach into the future. Be the people we want to be and help our communities be the best they can be. We often talk about lighting the darkness, and I believe our communities can provide that light. We can stand together to act for the betterment of all. We are community, we are family, our strength lies in our difference lets embrace

Simple actions by regular people can become important steps towards healing our communities and fostering safety and respect for everyone. After all our community is light. Our community is heart.

I believe there are several entities going on now that are enhancing community.

Religious communities are taking to social media, which is great. Mass is streamed, night reflections are proving very popular and priests from abroad are arriving to keep the flame burning.
Lay people are stepping forward to be trained, however there is still no bigger picture and very little action.

As this book goes to print Irish Bishops have embarked on 'The Synodal Pathway' leading to the holding of a National Synodal Assembly within the next five years. I see this as another 'kicking the can down the road' exercise. In this the Bishops foresee the next two years as a period of prayer, listening and discernment, involving a nationwide conversation on this theme. More conversation? Really?
This synod, the bishops say, will allow individuals and parishes, as well as organisations both within the Church, and Irish society, to share their insights into the Church in Ireland. It will include discussion and debate through information sessions and educational programmes on the meaning and processes of synodality. Will community members know what synodality means?

I feel language needs to be simpler more accessible. Also, how much discussion and debate do we need? It is so obvious what is happening right now. I agree that coming together is always good, but would it not be best to spend the next five years in action?

Community and caring for one another is key. Let's reach out, as never before, embrace our vocation to love one another.

Embrace the 'Priesthood of the Laity' the 'Priesthood of love'. Although not ministers of the altar, laity in all their actions of their everyday life can truly offer as much if not more than the priest, in their love and care for one another. The visionary aspect of the mission of the laity is to love one another as a parent loves their children. This adds to the priestly role of the laity in their community.

The laity live in the world and work in it, they imitate Christ who came among ordinary people in an ordinary life, in order to save us. We as lay people can save each other through love, care and reaching out.

For our own good, we need to equip the priesthood of the laity to celebrate the 'Liturgy of Community' in our homes, and to live a life of love and compassion in our work, our politics, our lives, and relationships. Almost 60 years after Vatican II, it's time to encourage the priesthood of the laity to grow. We are not second-class servants in the community. We are the core of all that is good and compassionate, we are the beating heart.

It is my opinion based on my solid experience that it will not be long before a priest will not be available to attend funerals so who will? It has been advised that deacons may lead the funeral liturgy and if a deacon is not available, a layperson with knowledge of the liturgy and traditions may lead the service. Therefore, through knowledge and love we may lay our dead to rest because we are the heart, hands, feet and face of the community and the world. We are the light and the heart.

St Flannans Cathedral Killaloe a haven of peace
(Photo Niamh Quinn)

Our Irish heritage has been passed down through stories and sympols which embody the love of our community. The Celtic cross is rich in powerful symbol of our hopes and dreams.

(By Niall Quinn)

About the Author

Marie O'Connell is an Irish author of short stories and press articles. She's the mother of three young adults, but she's also been a pastoral worker, a teacher, an administrator, a receptionist, a choir member, a dancer in an all-girl troupe, and a voice for women. She does her best writing in cafes, on park benches, on any beach, and at home in her community of Ballina/Killaloe. Marie loves to act, tell stories as well as write. She loved her time as a mature student where she graduated with a BA. A PG dip, an MA and she is about to pursue a PHD. In this book she transports her readers to a place where brave trailblazers guide communities to a new reality. Engaging communities to take responsibility where women and men are resilient and compassion is alive and well.

Cover design by Tara Quinn
Photos by Niamh Quinn
Photos by Kerry Blake
Sketch by Niall Quinn